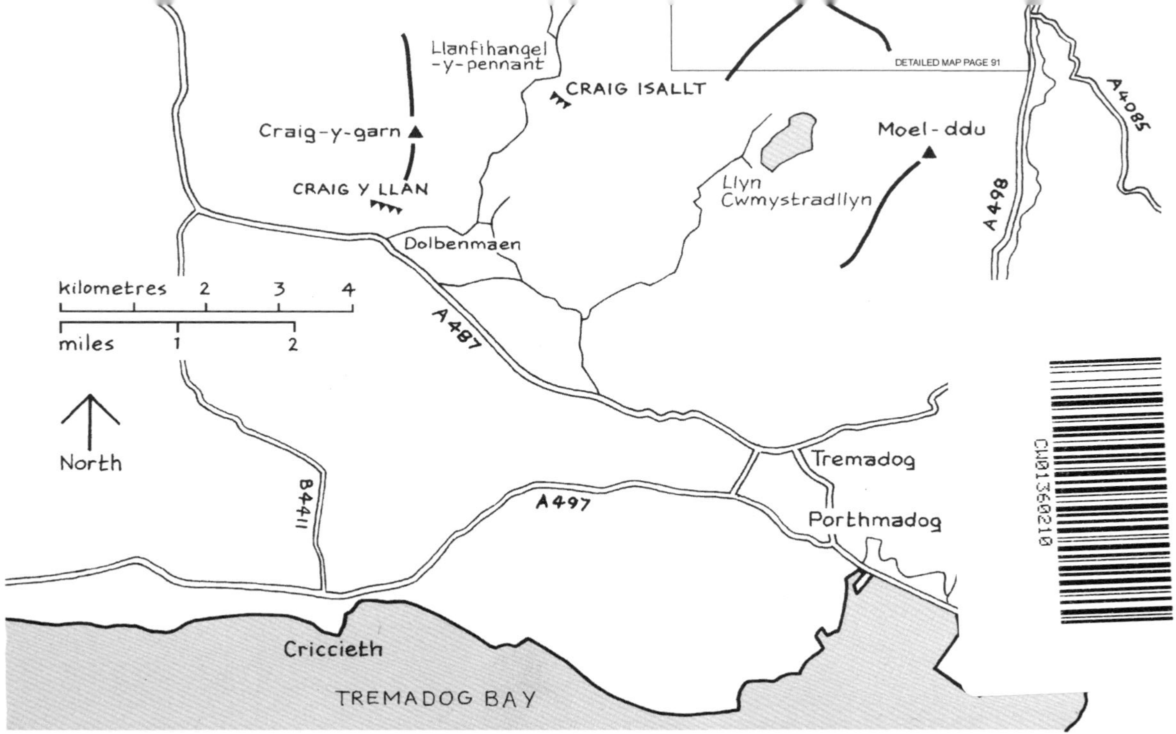
Llanfihangel
-y-pennant
CRAIG ISALLT
DETAILED MAP PAGE 91
A4085
Craig-y-garn
Moel-ddu
CRAIG Y LLAN
Llyn
Cwmystradllyn
A498
Dolbenmaen
kilometres 2 3 4
miles 1 2
A487
North
Tremadog
B4411
A497
Porthmadog
Criccieth
TREMADOG BAY

CW01360210

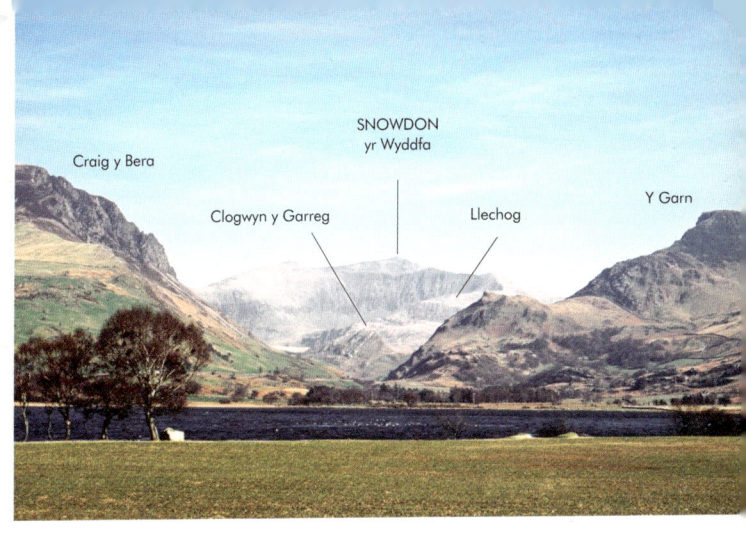

Dyffryn Nantlle and Snowdon from Llyn Nantlle Uchaf

photos: Don Sargeant

Cwm Silyn, the Nantlle Ridge, and Snowdon from the west

Climbers' Club Guides
Edited by John Willson

Cwm Silyn and Cwellyn
Rock and Winter Climbs in Eifionydd

by

Paul Jenkinson

and

Bob Wightman

Artwork

by

Don Sargeant

Published by The Climbers' Club

A Climber's Guide to Snowdon and the Beddgelert District (1926)
by Herbert R C Carr

Cwm Silyn and Cwellyn – First Edition (1971)
by Mike Yates and Jim Perrin

Tremadog and Cwm Silyn (1989)
by Mark Pretty, Dave Farrant, and Geoff Milburn

Cwm Silyn and Cwellyn (Eifionydd) – Second Edition (2003)
by Paul Jenkinson and Bob Wightman

© The Climbers' Club 2003

Jenkinson, Paul   Wightman, Bob   Cwm Silyn and Cwellyn (Eifionydd)
(Climbers' Club Guides)

British Library Cataloguing in Publication Data

A catalogue record for this book is available from the British Library

796.552

ISBN 0-901601-74-8

Front Cover: *Erection* (E2) Llechog
Climber: Nigel Coe
Photo: Don Sargeant

Rear Cover: *Balance of Power* (E5) Castell Cidwm
Climber: Pat Littlejohn
Photo: Littlejohn collection

Frontispiece: *Penates* (HVS) Craig yr Ogof
Climber: Paul Jenkinson
Photo: Don Sargeant

Typeset by the Editor
Slide Scanning by Redheads Digital, Sheffield
Produced by The Ernest Press, Glasgow G44 6AQ
Distributed by Cordee, 3a de Montfort Street, Leicester LE1 7HD

Contents

Editor's Note & Acknowledgements	8
Introduction	**10**
Historical	**16**
Cwellyn	**21**
Craig Cwm Du	21
Craig Cwm Bychan	27
Castell Cidwm	27
Llechog	37
Llechog Facet	46
Carreg Maen-bras	48
Craig Allt Maenderyn	48
Chwarel Ffridd Isaf	48
Dyffryn Nantlle & Cwm Silyn	**49**
Nantlle Slate Quarries	49
Twll Mawr	52
Craig y Bera	53
Clogwyn y Garreg	57
Y Garn	60
Llech Drws y Coed	62
Craig Trum y Ddysgl	63
Cwmffynnon	64
Cwm Silyn	65
Craig Lâs	65
Trwyn y Graig	66
Craig Fawr	69
Craig yr Ogof	70
Clogwyn y Cysgod	84
Craig Cwm Dulyn	87

Nant Colwyn — 90
- Castell — 90

Moel Hebog — 93
- The Summit Cliffs — 94
- Y Diffwys — 95
- The Rock of Ages — 99
- Y Braich — 99
- Y Braich Bach — 100

Cwm Pennant — 101
- Craig y Llan — 101
- Craig Isallt — 102
- Craig Cwm Trwsgl — 105

First Ascents — 111

Index of Climbs — 125

Index of Winter Climbs — 127

Accident Procedure — 128

Maps and Diagrams

Map of Guidebook Area	front endpaper
Craig Cwm Du ~ access map	20
Cwellyn ~ map	22
Castell Cidwm SE Face Left-hand Section*	32a
Castell Cidwm SE Face Central Section*	32b
Castell Cidwm SE Face Right-hand Section*	32c
Castell Cidwm ~ photoplan	32d
Llechog	48a
Llechog Facet	48d
Dyffryn Nantlle and Cwm Silyn ~ map	50
Craig y Bera	56b
Clogwyn y Garreg	56c
Llech Drws y Coed	56d
Cwm Silyn ~ photoplan	64a
Trwyn y Graig	64b
Craig Fawr and The Nose of Craig yr Ogof	72a
The West Wall of Craig yr Ogof	72b
The Great Slab of Craig yr Ogof	72c
Nant Colwyn and Cwm Pennant ~ map	91
Y Diffwys photodiagram	96a
Craig Cwm Trwsgl photodiagram	96b

*Photos by Alan Leary; all others by Don Sargeant

Climbers' Club Guides

The Climbers' Club
The publisher of this guidebook is The Climbers' Club, which was founded in 1898 from origins in Snowdonia and is now one of the foremost mountaineering clubs in Great Britain. Its objects are to encourage mountaineering and rock-climbing, and to promote the general interest of mountaineers and the mountain environment.

It is a truly national club with widespread membership, and currently owns huts in Cornwall, Pembrokeshire, Derbyshire, Snowdonia, and Argyll. Besides managing seven huts, The Climbers' Club produces an annual Journal and runs a full programme of climbing meets, dinners, and social events. Club members may also use the huts of other clubs through reciprocal arrangements. The club publishes climbing guidebooks (currently 20 in number) to cover most of Wales and Southern England. The club is a founder-member of, and is affiliated to, the British Mountaineering Council; it makes annual contributions to the Access and Conservation Trust, as well as to volunteer cliff and mountain rescue organizations. In 1999, the Climbers' Club Colin Kirkus Guidebook Fund was established as a means of distributing some of the profits earned from guidebooks to assist climbing-related projects that are in keeping with the aims of the club, though they need not be confined to the club's guidebook areas.

Membership fluctuates around 1,200, and at present there are no limits on growth. Members of two years' standing may propose a competent candidate for membership and, provided that adequate support is obtained from other members, the Committee may elect him or her to full membership; there is no probationary period.

Climbing Style
The following policy statement on climbing style was agreed in principle at The Climbers' Club Annual General Meeting on 25th February 1990:

The Climbers' Club supports the tradition of using natural protection and is opposed to actions which are against the best interest of climbers and users of the crags. This applies particularly to irreversible acts which could affect the crags and their environs.

Such acts could include: the placing of bolts on mountain and natural crags; retrospective placing of bolts; chiselling, hammering, or altering the rock appearance or structure; excessive removal of vegetation and interference with trees, flowers, and fauna.

The Climbers' Club policy is that guidebooks are written to reflect the best style matched to the ethos and traditions of British climbing.

The Climbers' Club Hut in Cwm Glas Mawr   Photo: Ian Smith

Guidebook Disclaimer

This guide attempts to provide a definitive record of all existing climbs and is compiled from information from a variety of sources. The inclusion of any route does not imply that it remains in the condition described. Climbs can change unpredictably: rock can deteriorate and the existence and condition of *in-situ* protection can alter. All climbers must rely on their own ability and experience to gauge the difficulty and seriousness of any climb. Climbing is an inherently dangerous activity.

Neither The Climbers' Club nor the authors and editor of this guidebook accept any liability whatsoever for any injury or damage caused to climbers, third parties, or property arising from the use of it. Whilst the content of the guide is believed to be accurate, no responsibility is accepted for any error, omission, or mis-statement. Users must rely on their own judgement and are recommended to insure against injury to person and property and third party risks.

The inclusion in this guidebook of a crag or routes upon it does not mean that any member of the public has a right of access to the crag or the right to climb upon it. Before climbing on any crag in this guidebook, please read the access and conservation notes in the Introduction (from page 12).

www.climbers-club.co.uk

Editor's Note & Acknowledgements

'By this Guide, which is intended to serve as a clue to a number of ascents distributed among the less-known and picturesque recesses of the Snowdon range, it is hoped that the balance may be something restored; and that, with its help, a few, at least, may discover in novelty, and not in excessive difficulty, in fresh external impression, and not in exaggerated personal sensation, lies the real romance of mountaineering adventure.'

'On a clear day in summer, the climber on Snowdon who looks towards the west rests his gaze on one of the most enchanting scenes in all Snowdonia. He is looking at an area of lakes and dark mysterious cwms, a land of legends. A remote area of small and shapely mountains, its crags an integral part of the mountain environment, it retains an atmosphere as timeless now as it was to Archer Thomson. … As a climbing-area it has a varied character and unique charm. It has never held the forefront in any intensive period of Welsh exploration but has steadily progressed to its present maturity.'

It was unexpectedly that I found myself editing this guide (during the 'secondment' of the Wales Editor to the club's Presidency) to a corner of Wales in which I had walked extensively in my early mountain days but had climbed barely at all. Reacquaintance fulfilled all anticipation, but equal reward and a greater surprise lay in coming across for the first time two earlier guidebooks to the area which, the more I delved, seemed the more to embody the very finest attributes of the genre in terms of reconciling clarity and accuracy with original and often inspirational expression, and of maintaining a valid and meaningful historical perspective in relation to the need to enable the climber to 'experience' the ascents. These are qualities that have always been elusive and are almost impossible to achieve today in the face of current obsession with E-points, stars, and multiple entries in first ascents columns. Even so, Eifionydd remains fortunate that its principal standard-bearers over its century's history have remained remote from this trait.

The first quotation above is taken from the Preface to Herbert Carr's 1926 *Climber's Guide to Snowdon and the Beddgelert District*, and is signed by Geoffrey Winthrop Young and the editorial team. The second is from the Introduction to *Cwm Silyn and Cwellyn* (1971) by Mike Yates and Jim Perrin. Each in its own way epitomizes what the hills and cwms and crags of Eifionydd have to offer. It is to the compilers of these two guides above all that the current team is indebted, though that is not to forget those responsible for various interim publications, and Dave Farrant, author of the Cwm Silyn section of the 1989 *Tremadog* guide.

I should like to express my personal appreciation of the forbearance of Paul Jenkinson and Bob Wightman, who produced scripts some years ago on the assumption that these would be incorporated within the plan of the overall

Tremadog–Meirionnydd structure, and then prepared to be paired off with *Clogwyn Du'r Arddu*. When it became apparent in the autumn of 2002 that the format plans for these were mutually incompatible it was decided to press ahead with a logical successor to the independent 1971 guide, and the pressure was on for the scripts to be fully revised and updated.

Many thanks to Barbara Jones of the Countryside Council for Wales for the Conservation Notes, and to Clare Bond, Access and Conservation Officer of the BMC, for the Geology Notes and for checking access arrangements with the Snowdonia National Park Authority.

Profound gratitude is due to Don Sargeant, who, after his marathon efforts in connection with *Meirionnydd* last year, is currently preparing the artwork for three other guides and assisting with a fourth, but has still found time to make repeated excursions into the hills to obtain satisfactory conditions to take the photos required and then to process all the artwork using the digital technology for the first time.

Thanks also to: Alan Leary for permission to use his splendid photos of Castell Cidwm; all those who have submitted action photos, especially Martin Whitaker, Terry Taylor, Pat Littlejohn, John Hartley, Ken Wilson, and of course Don again; and Ian Smith for the CGM hut photo, for organizing the scanning of the transparencies, and for the benefit of his technical advice and guidance throughout this first exercise in preparing all material for the printer in electronic form.

Finally, I must thank Ken Latham, Pat Littlejohn, Mike Lewis, Iwan Arfon Jones, and my fellow editors Bob Moulton and Nigel Coe for much general advice and encouragement and for reading and making helpful comments on the script, and John Cox and Mark Hounslea for performing that most thankless but essential of tasks: the formal proof-reading.

JW June 2003

I should like to thank: Pat Littlejohn, George Smith, Mike Lewis, Martin Crook, and Tom Leppert for providing information on their routes; Terry Taylor for being ever keen to develop esoterica in all weathers; and my wife, Karen, who has had to discover that a guidebook can't be written in a few hours and without recourse to the crags!

PJ June 2003

Solo work is rare these days, and my efforts are no exception. My thanks go to: Ken Latham and Jim Perrin for historical information; Mike Lynch for access to his personal library; Iwan Arfon Jones for many an interesting day on the hill; and finally Cath, my wife, who may now, just, see more of me!

REW June 2003

Introduction

Eifionydd
The mountains to the west of Yr Wyddfa in the north-western corner of Snowdonia are very popular with walkers but somewhat neglected by climbers. While the slabs of Cwm Silyn may attract a few climbers, it is not unusual to be alone on Llechog on a sunny Saturday in July. For many, the peace and solitude are the best aspect of the climbing in Eifionydd.

The climbing is concentrated in the four principal valleys that make up the area. **Dyffryn Nantlle** is home to the mountain crags of Cwm Silyn, the ramparts of Craig y Bera, the quarry routes near Talysarn, and the roadside outcrops of Drws y Coed and Clogwyn y Garreg. In the quiet and peaceful **Cwm Pennant**, Craig Cwm Trwsgl and Craig Isallt are found. **Nant y Betws** is the valley in which Llyn Cwellyn is located, with the mighty Castell Cidwm rearing up from the shores of the lake. South of Pont Cae'r-gors, the valley that leads to Beddgelert is called **Nant Colwyn**, and here are the high mountain crags of Moel Hebog along with the delightful outcrops of Castell.

The variety of the climbing that the area offers is outstanding: routes of all types and standards are to be found in many contrasting settings and locations, and on both low-lying and high-mountain crags. There is also a smattering of bolt routes in the slate quarries, though they can't compete in quality with those of the Llanberis quarries.

The historical importance of the area should not be ignored, as many of the great pioneers of Welsh climbing from Mallory to Fawcett have cut their teeth in the area. On the summit cliffs of Moel Hebog is the Simdde'r Foel where Owain Glyndŵr is said to have climbed to evade the English army in the early fifteenth century.

Whatever your passion, the area will have something for you all. But remember it's often a lonely place to be, so come prepared and you will be able to enjoy one of the forgotten corners of Welsh climbing to the full.

Approach and Topography
The climbing is situated on either side of the A4085 and radiates from the hub of Rhyd Ddu, not quite midway between Beddgelert and Caernarfon. Rhyd Ddu is reached:
- by taking the North Coast route to Caernarfon and then driving south;
- or by turning left off the A5 at Capel Curig, and going straight on at Pen y Gwryd (instead of turning right for the Pass) to Beddgelert;
- or via the moorland minor road from 3 miles north-west of Llanberis across to Waunfawr.

The exception is Cwm Pennant: a minor road runs up the valley from the A487 (the more direct link between Porthmadog and Caernarfon) from just west of Tremadog. The A487 may also provide a slightly shorter approach to Cwm Silyn, depending upon starting-point.

There is a large National Park car-park in Rhyd Ddu (pay and display £2 in 2003), and (currently) free parking two kilometres to the north at Snowdon Ranger and a similar distance to the south near the entrance to the Forestry tracks at Pont Cae'r Gors. There is a convenient pub in the village, but no shop, café, or petrol-station.

There are numerous campsites up and down the A4085. The Forestry Commission site at OS Ref 579 491 is popular with caravans, and usually requires pre-booking for weekends in summer. Better bets are Cae Du in Beddgelert (OS Ref 597 486) and the Snowdonia Park Hotel in Waunfawr (OS Ref 526 587), the latter being next to a family-friendly pub.

The guidebook is organized to follow three clockwise arcs or circles, from north to south: the first forms a ring around Llyn Cwellyn; the second loops around Dyffryn Nantlle; and the third goes down Nant Colwyn, over Moel Hebog, and back up Cwm Pennant.

The technical geology of the region is explained below but the rocks are of volcanic types that will appear reasonably familiar to mainstream North Wales climbers; limestone is nowhere to be found. The weather is, of course, just as fickle as in the highest Snowdonia peaks; but, being a few metres lower and a few kilometres nearer the sea, the area may just escape its most extreme manifestations of harshness, and it is well worth noting that the average annual rainfall over Nantlle is less than half that at Pen y Gwryd. The corollary, though, is that vegetation finds it that much easier to thrive, and some of the older and less-frequented climbs may no longer seem the 'classics' they were once 'destined to be'.

Geology
by Clare Bond

Snowdonia 470 to 450 million years ago (in the Ordovician period) was a sea out of which rose large volcanoes. This activity, with the muds and silts of the sea floor, formed most of the rocks we see today in the area; though the slates of Dyffryn Nantlle and Llanberis form part of a sequence of Cambrian rocks deposited between 570 and 500 million years ago in environments ranging from deep ocean basins to shallow marine areas of silts and muds. The Ordovician activity was the result of a phase of tectonic processes which closed the ocean, and folded and metamorphosed the rocks. Large north-to-north-east-trending faults divided the region into a series of blocks that slid past each other, squashing together and folding the sediments and tuffs. Minerals, such as copper, lead, and zinc, were deposited during the volcanism in fractures that formed as water was heated and forced through the rock.

The rocks of the Cwm Silyn massif are made of muds and siltstones overlain by welded acid tuffs – acid meaning that the rock contains pale minerals with a high content of silica. The tuff has formed from large volcanic ash flows, like those seen recently on the island of Montserrat, and the welding is the result of the immensely high temperature of the ash as it is erupted, which forms plumes and flows to give a layered appearance. The Cwm Silyn tuffs seem to have been trapped in a large caldera or other confined space within the volcanic terrain, rather than to have flowed over long distances. Some of the Ordovician sediments have also formed slate, such as that mined in Ffestiniog: the sediments are inter-layered with volcanic tuff and intruded by igneous rocks, including dolerite and the micro-granite of Craig Cwm Bychan. Elsewhere in the area, the sediments show a greater variety of depositional environments, from deep to shallow marine. Those of Moel Hebog are sandstones, some containing pebbles, suggesting a near-shore environment, with deltas and rivers carrying sediment down into the sea from the flanks of the volcanoes. Here the sandstone is inter-bedded with tuffs and also intruded by dolerite.

The current landscape was 'carved' during the last glacial period, between 27,000 and 10,000 years ago, to give the wonderful U-shaped valleys of Ogwen and the high cwms such as Cwm Silyn, with their fine climbing-cliffs. The ice also carried large boulders ('erratics'), for those who prefer bouldering. This landscape has since been modified by human activity such as farming and, interestingly from a geological point of view, mining. Mining of the local slate has probably taken place since Roman times, whilst small-scale mining for minerals from veins and fractures occurred in the nineteenth and early twentieth centuries.

Winter Climbing in Eifionydd
Winter climbing in the area, like its summer cousin, is something of a backwater in modern times – Ogwen or the Trinity Face it isn't. The closeness of the sea and its climatic influence mean that a severe winter is required for many of the cliffs and climbs to come into condition; but when such conditions do occur there are a number of excellent courses available. In particular, the crags of Craig Cwm Dulyn offer several ice-climbs in the middle grades only a few minutes from the road. The other main centre is Clogwyn y Cysgod in Cwm Silyn. The remainder of the recorded lines are scattered around the area; often a whole cwm offers only one or two climbs.

Most winter lines are of the 'classic' variety; that is, they require a substantial covering of snow and/or ice. The modern predilection for thinly iced 'mixed' climbing has not yet manifested itself here. It is to be hoped that any prospective lines are attempted in as good a style as possible and **no damage** should be caused to summer lines.

Access
Please note the statement in bold-print at the bottom of page 7. There have been considerable difficulties over the years around Mynydd Mawr and Castell Cidwm, and also below Y Garn at the eastern end of the Nantlle Ridge, and so it is vital to use the approaches described and avoid any

antagonism. Llechog Facet has been the scene of some confrontation in the past, but it is thought that this has now been solved. Access to Clogwyn y Garreg and Craig Isallt is problematic, but things may change with the full implementation of CRoW (see below).

Y Garn and Trum y Ddysgl are the only crags subject to a bird restriction, and that a rather unusual one (see pages 14 and 60). Please co-operate.

There is a general presumption that once open ground (i.e. uncultivated land) is legitimately reached (by right-of-way or permitted path) that it is all right to wander anywhere provided no damage is caused or threatened to livestock or constructions. However, this is not a statutory right. Trespass on private (including open) land, even where there is no evidence of prohibition, is a civil tort and anyone asked to leave by a landowner or official in authority should be prepared to do so. Please report such an incident promptly to the BMC's Access and Conservation Officer, who will know best how to resolve the matter.

The Countryside and Rights of Way Act (known universally as CRoW) received the royal assent in 2000, but its provisions with regard to open access are unlikely to take significant effect before c.2005. From then, the 'right to roam' (which includes the climbing of rocks) on much open land (but not, of course, cultivated farmland) will become statutory, though may still be subject to various conditions and limitations (which in certain circumstances could be *more* restrictive than the current *de-facto* position). At that stage, climbers are strongly urged not to make any general assumptions without obtaining precise clarification of individual circumstances. It is expected that the BMC will provide full information and guidance, and The Climbers' Club will endeavour to publish on its website the ways in which individual crags or climbing areas covered by its guidebooks will be affected.

It should scarcely be necessary to enjoin climbers to observe the Country Code, especially with regard to: leaving litter; damage to walls or fences; leaving gates open; lighting fires; controlling dogs; parking considerately; harming wildlife or vegetation; and disturbing sheep, especially in the lambing season (February to April).

Conservation *by Barbara Jones*

The area covered by this guide is large and varied. Situated on the western edge of northern Snowdonia, the hills are lower and less dramatic than the mountains to the east. They tend to be subject to a more maritime influence and in places support somewhat more heath than further east in Eryri, possibly as a result of less grazing and the rather more equable climate. The geology is varied but has fewer of the more base-rich rock intrusions which characterize a number of the large cliffs of central Snowdonia. The more acidic nature of the cliffs and their generally lower altitude means that they tend to support widespread heath and grass species rather than the rarer alpine type of flora. This doesn't apply to all cliffs in this guide, however, with wet gullies on Craig Cwm Du, Mynydd Drws y Coed, Craig Cwm Silyn, and

Llechog supporting fern- and-herb rich vegetation such as starry saxifrage, globeflower, roseroot, and great woodrush.

The cliffs to the north of Moel Hebog are important botanically. They tend to be well vegetated, probably explaining why few routes have been recorded there. However, there are some stretches of less vegetated, but loose, rock on these cliffs, which may attract the more adventurous; but *please* contact CCW before undertaking any exploration here as we stand to lose a great deal if plants are removed from this location.

The Dyffryn Nantlle area is noted for the bird life it supports. This is particularly the case on Y Garn and Trum y Ddysgl, which are important roosting-sites for chough, and the introductory paragraphs to these two cliffs include information on how to avoid disturbing these birds during their roosting season. This involves a request to avoid climbing at these sites from one hour before sunset until sunrise, from August to November inclusive, when the birds need to have undisturbed access to the cliffs. Getting down from your climb an hour before dark is a small price to pay to see the skydiving antics of this wonderful bird. There is also a regularly used nest site on Moel Hebog close to the climbing crags, so if you do see agitated birds during the breeding-season of April to June, then please stay clear of any active nest site.

RSPB and CCW would be glad to hear of any records of nesting chough, dead choughs, or parts of birds, with or without rings, or any flocks, especially of birds on the ground rather than high fly-overs, from anywhere in this area. This information is helping to build up a picture of the breeding success and movements of this bird in Snowdonia, which is one of its strongholds in the UK. Information is most useful if it includes a date and a grid reference or 1 km square, and if it is received as soon after the sighting as possible, although older information can also be useful. The RSPB contact number is 01248 363800.

There are a number of special sites in this area, some designated for their botanical importance and some for their geological interest. Examples include pollen preserved in the muds, clays, and peats near Clogwyn y Garreg, which allow scientists to reconstruct the environmental conditions and plant types that have lived in the area during the last 14,000 years or so. Rocks at Trum y Ddysgl have been folded and fractured and the Cambrian strata have been overturned and thrust south-eastwards over the younger Ordovician rocks. Llyn Cwellyn and Afon Gwyrfai are internationally important for the freshwater habitats and species they support; and bats, water voles, and otters can be found in Dyffryn Nantlle.

So although this area may be less spectacular than the mountains to the east, it has its own conservation and landscape interest. If you want specific information on any particular conservation interest of the area, contact the Countryside Council for Wales Area Office on 01248 672500.

Equipment

The crags of Llechog, Moel Hebog, and Cwm Silyn all lie around or above the 600-metre contour, with a walk in of the best part of an hour or more. It is thus advisable to be fully equipped with hill-walking gear, including waterproofs, adequate footwear, and map and compass.

The 1:50,000 OS Landranger map 115 (Caernarfon) and 1:25,000 Outdoor Leisure map 17 (Snowdon & Conwy Valley) both cover the whole guidebook area except for the minor crag of Crag y Llan at the bottom of Cwm Pennant.

The Guidebook

Every effort has been made to render the book as user-friendly as possible, notably by a full provision and careful placement of maps and diagrams, and the insertion of several cross-references. A map or diagram can generally be expected to be found within two pages of the start of the section to which it is a guide; where that has not been practicable, the page number is noted.

The grades used are the standard ones, and an effort has been made to supply technical grades (4a and above) for Severes and Hard Severes, for the first time on a number of crags, though a few still elude.

A dagger symbol † is used to show that a route is not known to have had a second ascent (at least in a style comparable with or better than the first). Unfortunately, records are not comprehensive in this respect.

[R] on a route-title line indicates that a part-time access restriction applies.

Left and right are always used as if facing the crag, even in descent, unless otherwise stated.

The usual three-star system has been used to denote the authors' evaluation of route quality, taking due account of tradition. The underlying assumption when attributing stars has been that all routes described in full have merit and are worthy of visiting climbers' attention unless it is explicitly noted otherwise. Thus all starred routes are of significantly above-average quality. If a recent or unrepeated route is claimed by the first ascensionist to be of quality, then hollow stars are used (and it is hoped that a consensus can be reached before the next edition of the guide); these are always unmodified by the author.

Where Welsh names for the crags are known they are used, and translations are generally placed after them on the heading lines. Often, the literal translations can appear cryptic or meaningless in the context and some imagination is needed to supply the metaphorical link; and a few arbitrary decisions have had to be taken in the choice of alternatives.

New routes and perhaps new crags will continue to be found in this region. The normal repository for North Wales new-route descriptions is the Pete's Eats log book in Llanberis, email info@petes-eats.co.uk; and details of new routes etc. can be found on the Pete's Eats website: www.petes-eats.co.uk.

Historical

1400 – 1926

The area to the south and west of Yr Wyddfa (Snowdon) is home to many early Celtic hill-forts, and it is tempting to imagine the occupants moving among the high and rocky places in search of prey.

A tale from around 1400 concerns one such prey: a certain Owain Glyndŵr. On the run from a company of the English army, he climbed Simdde'r Foel Hebog before fleeing across the summit of Moel Hebog to hide in a cave on Moel yr Ogof for six months, sustained by supplies from the Prior of Beddgelert.

Early exploration of the area in the modern sense was mainly in the form of attaining the peaks and traversing the ridges. At the start of the twentieth century, attention turned to the rocks themselves with W P Haskett Smith to the fore in recording the first true climbs in 1905, the best of which is the striking *Eastern Arête* on Y Garn. Given the amount of rock patently around, it is surprising that he did not record more.

The redoubtable J M Archer Thomson was next to take up the reins. Along with Haskett Smith and H O Jones, he initiated a sustained development of Llechog and Cwm Du. Thomson enthused about Llechog, but the rock at the latter venue was noted for its lack of quality. The highlight of this period was the ascent by Harold Porter and George Mallory of the central ridge of Y Garn: *Mallory's Ridge*. Even by the first ascent it had acquired a reputation, following the death of Anton Stoop on an earlier attempt. It would be forty years before it was repeated, and it must be one of the earliest climbs in Wales to warrant the modern HVS grade.

Attention was slowly turning to the Cwm Silyn cliffs. *Sunset Rib* from before the Great War was the first, but it had to wait twelve years until the ascent of *Overhanging Chimneys* on Trwyn y Graig for a companion. Trwyn y Graig was virtually worked out in the space of a year before thought was given to the crags to the right. Herbert Carr, who had been involved in the first ascents of many of the Trwyn y Graig climbs, including *Overhanging Chimneys*, began the process with *Artist's Climb*, *Amphitheatre Buttress*, and *Nirvana Wall*. But it was left to David Pye to show the possibilities of the Great Slab of Craig yr Ogof with *Ordinary Route* (originally known as *The Great Slab Route*) in 1926. Carr had also been collating information on the existing climbs in the area, and in that year the third of the Climbers' Club 'pocket guides' appeared: *A Climber's Guide to Snowdon and the Beddgelert District*.

The Erg (E5), Castell Cidwm (first ascent, 1965)
Climber: John Clements   Photo: John Hartley (Bâton Wicks archive)

Eureka (E1), Craig yr Ogof (first ascent, 1966)
Climber: Laurie Holliwell   Photo: Ken Wilson

1927 – 1971

Five years later came two climbers who, in their different ways, have each left a lasting impression on the cliffs of Wales, and each put up a route that has stood the test of time. First on the scene was Colin Kirkus, who ascended the centre of the Great Slab to produce one of the most elegant climbs in the district. Originally named *Right Hand Route* it is more usually known as *Kirkus's Climb*. The other was the tortured soul of Menlove Edwards, who struck out left from the slab to ascend *Outside Edge Route*. Perhaps more to his liking were his peregrinations on the other side of the cwm on Clogwyn y Cysgod, but unlike *Outside Edge Route* these have never been popular.

The Second World War now intervened and halted development, but cessation of hostilities saw new names appearing in the first ascents roster. Tony Moulam visited Craig y Bera on several occasions to claim new lines, his first and best being *Angel Pavement*, which takes the prominent slab of good rock on the main central buttress. Moulam later visited Cwm Silyn to climb *Ogof Direct* with what could have been one of the largest first-ascent parties ever seen. Fortunately for guidebook writers, most of the group were 'lost' during the ascent.

The summit cliffs of Moel Hebog saw steady if unspectacular development, mainly by Paul Work, but the crag has not become popular.

The only climb of real note during the mid 50s was the aided line of *Bourdillon's Climb* on Craig yr Ogof.

As plans for new guidebooks took shape, Joe Brown visited the area searching for yet another 'crag X' and, acting on a vague recollection of Claude Davies, stumbled upon Castell Cidwm. Hardly able to believe his luck, he attempted the line of *Dwm*, but had to return to complete it with Harold Smith. Brown's eye for a line saw him complete two further routes on the forbidding wall to the left of *Dwm*: *Vertigo* and *The Curver* are fine examples of route-finding through improbable terrain.

The first *Snowdon South* guide was published in 1960, but *Snowdon East* had to wait a decade and *Snowdon West* (robbed of Clogwyn Du'r Arddu which was allotted its own volume) never came to fruition. However, development continued with a stunner: *Tramgo* on Castell Cidwm. The first ascent of this unrelentingly steep crackline to the right of *Dwm* came complete with tales of hanging horizontally from fist-jams and the leader being unable to raise his arms above his head after the ascent. That leader, of course, was Brown. Though the ascent required some aid, it was a major breakthrough and the route has seen few ascents since.

Unclimbed rock appeared to be in short supply, but one challenge stood out: the West Wall of the Ogof Nose at Cwm Silyn. Hugh Banner, amongst others, had made several attempts, though it was Baz Ingle who finally solved the route-finding problems to produce *Crucible*. Ingle then continued sporadic development of the Cwm Silyn cliffs throughout the 60s, leaving *Desifinado*, *Aquarius,* and *Brutus* as marks of his passage.

With the attention on Cwm Silyn, Castell Cidwm saw little activity other than Jim Swallow's *The Straighter* until the arrival of John Clements. *Glwm* in 1964 was first, but the daunting *Central Wall* a week later was better. The following year saw effort being expended on *The Erg* before the 'last great problem' of the *Cidwm Girdle* was solved. All these ascents involved some aid, but this was very much in the style of the time and the lines being attempted were intimidating to say the least. Tragically, Clements was killed later that year in Glencoe. Cidwm would have to wait a long time for new challengers.

Back at Cwm Silyn, outsiders to the established order arrived keen to make their mark. First were the Holliwells with *Eureka,* a bold direct line through *Crucible*. However, they did not press their advantage, and left for the delights [?] of Llech Ddu. That marauding Lancastrian, Ray Evans, made more of a mark with *Codswallop* and *Jabberwocky*, the latter climbed in old RAF boots! Proof that the Gully Era had not been left behind may be found in the ascent, by Mike and Judy Yates, of *Green Gully*, perhaps the hardest of its kind in Snowdonia.

Elsewhere, and to demonstrate that the area is not just about Cidwm and Cwm Silyn, Jim Perrin finally solved the mystery of Archer Thomson's 'gaunt red crag' and came up with the fine *Resurrection* on Llechog, though the final section was avoided. Evans also searched out and completed the oft-tried *Dulyn Groove* on Craig Cwm Dulyn, though with some mild controversy as he used more aid than those parties who had failed.

1971 – 1989

The arrival of the first guidebook devoted exclusively to the area did not produce the expected rush for new lines. Indeed, the next decade saw only a handful being recorded on the main cliffs. It was to be at Craig Cwm Trwsgl that the first significant development took place.

This previously ignored cliff at the head of Cwm Pennant was developed in the main by Perrin. He began with the best route on the crag, *The Exterminating Angel*, but curiously ignored the remaining possibilities of this buttress and moved along the cliff to produce a series of routes that have remained largely neglected.

Noteworthy around this time was the removal of the last aid point at Cwm Silyn, with *Atropos* going free to R Townshend. Routes previously ascended with aid such as *Brutus* and *Jabberwocky* had received free ascents by various parties without claims being made. *Dulyn Groove* was the final route in the valley to be freed of its aid, by Mick Fowler in 1982.

In 1974 Ken Latham and friends began the development of the crag with easiest access hereabouts: Llech Drws y Coed. This had certainly been climbed on before, mainly, it appears, as an aid practice-ground, but few details have been unearthed.

Castell Cidwm had lain dormant during this period, but its remaining offerings were obvious to those who dared to look. *Tramgo* was free climbed by Jim Moran in 1978, *Zwm* followed in 1979, and the following year the first of the remaining big lines was to go. *Hang 'em High,* the crackline up the steep wall to the right of *Tramgo* needed a big effort on an early-season day, and this was superbly provided by Moran again; but the 'Free the Pass' campaign initiated by Geoff Milburn, his partner on both these routes, beckoned, and he did not return. Another energy-sapping pitch also came into being this year with Ron Fawcett's free ascent of *The Erg*. However, it was to be a further eight years before Cidwm truly met its match.

Never the most popular of crags, Llechog had to wait for the arrival of Banner and the Yateses to complete the true finish to *Resurrection* with the technical *Erection*. They had previously climbed *Blood on the Tracks* and *Slopey,* and finished this wave of exploration with *Zarquon*. (This latter has since seen some damage following attempts at a winter ascent.)

On a lesser scale from this time were the first explorations of the slate quarries around the village of Nantlle, John Sylvester taking the honours here with his ascent of the technical *Oars Moses* in Twll Mawr.

A late development in this era took place back on Craig Cwm Trwsgl where Dai Lampard and Al Phizacklea took advantage of Perrin's former neglect to produce four new lines, of which the best are *Day of Reckoning* and *The Seraphic Sanction*.

Finally, in 1988, Cidwm's nemesis came in the form of Pat Littlejohn, who, obviously climbing well, set about the lines of 'weakness' left on the main wall. He eventually departed with seven new routes under his belt, partnered mostly by Jon de Monytjoye and Steve Monks. All were of some difficulty, but *Potency* and *Light Years* were outstanding: technical, strenuous, and bold.

1989 – 2003

Again, the appearance of a new guide, 'Cwm Silyn' tacked onto the back of *Tremadog,* did little to galvanize new activity; the area did not seem to appeal to the modern generation.

At Castell Cidwm, few appeared willing to take up the challenges remaining after the work of Littlejohn, most being content with repeating and confirming the quality, and difficulty, of the existing lines. One that did was Mike Turner, who commenced work on the crackline to the right of *Hang 'em High*. After considerable effort spread over several days, *Howl at the Moon* came into being. Also receiving attention here was the obvious direct finish to *Dwm*. This attracted many suitors until in the end Sean Myles, on fine form, finally broke through the *Freedwm Roof*.

Throughout the 80s several of the crags omitted from previous guides were 'discovered': Chris Parkin and George Smith developed Llech Drws y Coed, unaware of the earlier work, and added several routes that were new. Mike

Lewis visited the Nantlle quarries and developed the dolerite ribs and grooves in Twll Mawr, in the process rediscovering the line climbed by Sylvester. Other quarries have been developed, but in general the quality of both the rock and the climbs here is not up to that in the Llanberis quarries.

After bringing Castell Cidwm into the modern era, Pat Littlejohn was keen to do the same for another traditional crag: Craig y Bera. He began by accepting the challenge thrown down in the 1989 guide to climb *The Sceptic* at a surprisingly amenable grade. He then proceeded to develop the walls above and below the main slab of *Angel Pavement* with a series of ever more difficult climbs. Not everyone has found the rock here attractive, and the lines have so far seen much less attention than his efforts at Cidwm.

It was left to Zdiszlaw (Tom) Leppert to produce perhaps the most surprising development, that of Llechog Facet. Lying below the outfall of Cwm Clogwyn, the bluffs are seen only at a distance, from the Snowdon Ranger path. Working in secret, and with most of the locals thinking that his 'new' crag was in the Carneddau, Tom and various partners climbed a series of powerful routes worthy of attention.

Having played a major part in the modern development of two of the area's main cliffs, and with Cwm Silyn all but worked out, Littlejohn let the development of Llechog slip through his hands. Benefiting from this largesse, Lewis, (Judy) Yates, Kelvin Neal, and Jeff Hope in various combinations accrued a haul of fourteen routes on the scattered buttresses of this rarely visited cliff, thus appropriately bringing the wheel full circle to Thomson's starting-point.

Most recently, there have been developments on the smaller buttresses above the edges of Beddgelert forest along with cliffs such as Clogwyn y Garreg at the head of Dyffryn Nantlle. These would appear to be a mopping-up operation until those with the eye, and the ability, see the remaining lines.

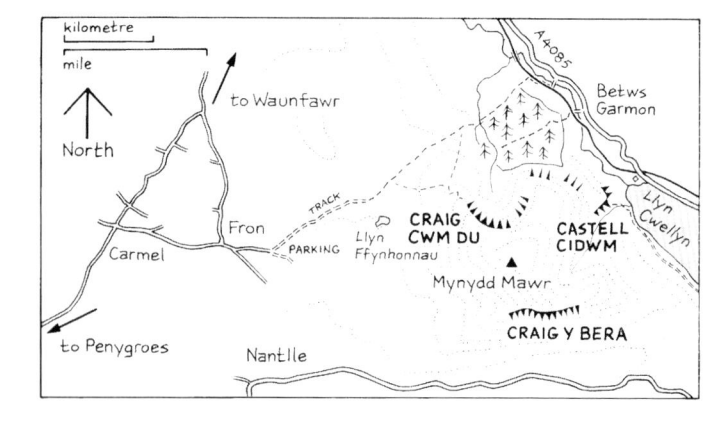

Cwellyn

Craig Cwm Du   Black Hollow Crag   OS Ref 537 551

This dark shadowy crag looms large above the Waunfawr to Betws Garmon road. It is a quiet place where one is unlikely to see other climbers, who may be put off by the walk, the north-facing aspect, and the fact that the base of the crag is over 450 metres above sea-level. Despite the lack of quality of some of the climbing, the crag has a number of lower-grade routes of a distinct mountaineering character. *Adam Rib* stands out as one of the classic mountaineering routes of the whole of Snowdonia.

The cliff dominates the cwm. On the left-hand side is the wide broken area of the Eastern Cliffs. Further right is the more substantial Eden Buttress with the prominent right arête taken by *Adam Rib*. Eden Gully separates this buttress from the more extensive Fluted Buttress, which is split by a large heather terrace. Beyond another gully is the largest section, the Central Cliff, again divided into an upper and lower tier. Right again past two further gullies are the vegetated Western Slabs.

Three distinct approaches to the crag are possible (see opposite). The recommended (and quickest – 30 minutes) is from Fron. Follow the road through the village, fork left up into the quarry, and park by the quarry buildings (OS Ref 513 548). Walk along the road, which soon becomes a track; then take the path eastwards onto the crest of the ridge, from where the crag can be clearly seen in the cwm to the right.

Alternatively, from Betws Garmon, cross the bridge at OS Ref 544 567 and take the path west, then south-west by the edge of the forest. Once the fields are passed, walk south up the ridge to meet the path from Fron.

Finally, a public footpath leaves the road just to the south (OS Ref 546 563) and leads up steeply through the forest to reach open ground. Then take an obvious line to the crag.

Many of the climbs finish close to the summit of Mynydd Mawr, so the mountaineering flavour of the cliffs can easily be enhanced with a summit experience. On a clear day the whole of the Eifionydd area and beyond can be seen.

The simplest descent is by the path on the western side of the cliff. It is also possible to descend a couple of the gullies if you are a devotee of all things botanical. The first begins down Saxifrage Gully (page 24), gained by going down rightwards (facing out) from the broken area at the top of the Central Cliff, and then follows the grassy slopes of Central Rake on the left at half height before regaining the gully. Alternatively, follow the Central Rake (which connects the two gullies) in its entirety, reached by descending the top of *Grass Pitch Gully* (page 26). Great care is required with these two descents, but they do allow a close look at the immediate cliff environment.

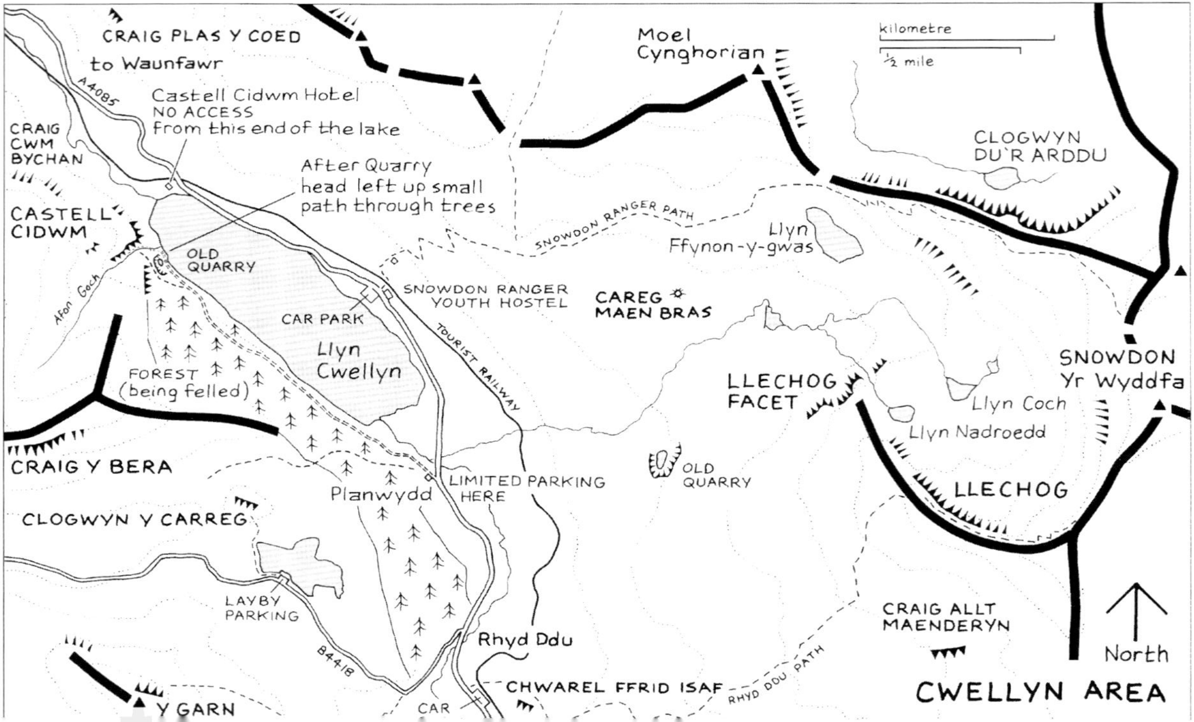
CRAIG PLAS Y COED
to Waunfawr
A4085
Castell Cidwm Hotel
NO ACCESS
from this end of the lake
CRAIG
CWM
BYCHAN
After Quarry
head left up small
path through trees
CASTELL
CIDWM
OLD
QUARRY
Afon Goch
CAR PARK
Llyn
Cwellyn
FOREST
(being felled)
CRAIG Y BERA
Planwydd
CLOGWYN Y CARREG
LAYBY
PARKING
B4418
Y GARN
CAR
Rhyd Ddu
CHWAREL FFRID ISAF
LIMITED PARKING
HERE
TOURIST RAILWAY
SNOWDON RANGER
YOUTH HOSTEL
SNOWDON RANGER PATH
CAREG
MAEN BRAS
OLD
QUARRY
Moel
Cynghorian
kilometre
½ mile
Llyn
Ffynon-y-gwas
CLOGWYN
DU'R ARDDU
LLECHOG
FACET
Llyn Nadroedd
Llyn Coch
SNOWDON
Yr Wyddfa
LLECHOG
RHYD DDU PATH
CRAIG ALLT
MAENDERYN
North
CWELLYN AREA

The Eastern Cliffs

This large and broken cliff on the left-hand side provides entertaining scrambles on and around the prominent Crazy Pinnacle. The only recorded route here is rather loose.

Jezebel 50 metres Very Difficult (12.8.38)
Climb the rib immediately left of the pinnacle.

Eden Buttress

The cliff now asserts itself in this steep, slender buttress, its prominent right arête giving the best route of the crag.

Eve's Folly 81 metres Difficult (29.12.49)
A reasonable route, somewhat overshadowed by its more illustrious neighbour. Start by scrambling up to the foot of the broad left-hand rib of the buttress.
1 12m. Move up to a ledge from the left, climb over the perched block above, and follow a crack to a grassy ledge.
2 21m. Gain the grassy ledge on the left; then follow the rib on the right to a large grassy ledge.
3 27m. Scrambling leads to another grassy ledge beneath an overhang. Belay by a small cave on the right.
4 21m. Climb the nose above the cave from the left; then go rightwards to a ledge. Step right round the rib and go diagonally right to finish.

★★**Adam Rib** 121 metres Hard Severe (1911)
This route takes the right arête of Eden Buttress and gives impressive and interesting climbing. Start at the foot of the right-hand rib, just left of Eden Gully.
1 46m. Easy climbing leads to a grassy ledge, where the rib steepens.
2 27m. Move into the wide groove on the left and climb its left wall to gain a subsidiary rib on the left. Follow this to an obvious traverse back right onto the main rib at another grassy ledge. Alternatively, climb the groove on the right of the stance to gain the main rib and follow this with interest to the same stance.
3 27m. Take the cracks left of the edge to easier climbing and a small ledge. Move left and go up to a small stance.
4 21m. Gain the exposed and narrow rib from the right, treating the rock with respect, and follow the rib in a splendid position to the top.

Eden Gully is the wet gully to the right: enter at your peril.

Fluted Buttress

Right again, a wider buttress is split at mid height by a large heather terrace.

★Knight's Move Climb   135 metres   Very Difficult   (1911)
A good route taking a zigzag line up the cleanest part of the lower section of the buttress to finish up the obvious ridge on its right-hand edge. Start at the foot of the slabs at the left edge of the buttress.
1 30m. Climb up leftwards to a ledge on the left edge, and then follow the groove on the right to a grassy ledge on the left.
2 15m. Move back right onto the arête; then follow ledges round to the heather terrace.
3 30m. Go easily up right to the edge overlooking Saxifrage Gully and continue to a small stance just left of a minor gully.
4 30m. Follow the ridge above to a ledge; then move round left, up a metre or so, and back right to a grassy ledge (The Knight's Move). Climb a short wall to grass, and ascend this to a belay at some large spikes.
5 30m. Move up to a small bay on the right and climb another short wall; scrambling remains.
Variations
1a An inferior direct start is possible up the right-hand edge of the buttress to an overhang at 30 metres; then take the groove on the right to the heather terrace.
4a Join the minor gully (Kershaw's Gully) by a traverse right 3 metres above the stance, and follow the gully until the original route is rejoined.

Saxifrage Gully is the wet gully to the right and provides a possible descent route. About 30 metres up the gully is the start of the Central Rake. This splits the Central Cliff and provides access to the routes on the upper part.

Upper Central Cliff
A rather broken cliff littered with ledges and grooves. It is most continuous on the left where the two routes exist. Both start on a terrace that runs from the Central Rake into Saxifrage Gully some 60 metres up. A grassy recess some 12 metres up, reached by the routes, is another landmark.

Poverty Street   83 metres   Very Severe   (30.5.70)
Start on the terrace, at the foot of the first groove right of the gully.
1 12m. Climb the groove into a steep corner. Hand-traverse left on poor rock and climb the bulge above; then move rightwards into the grassy recess.
2 37m. Traverse left between the two sets of overhangs to reach a thin crack and follow this to a large terrace.
3 34m. Climb the crack to the top.

Medicare   86 metres   Severe   (30.5.70)
Better than *Poverty Street*. Start at a groove 5 metres to its right.
1 12m. Climb the groove direct to the grassy recess.
2 40m. Move right for 3 metres, and then go through the overhangs into a scoop. Climb this and easier rock to the grassy terrace.
3 34m. Move across to the rib, which provides the finish.

Lower Central Cliff

This, the largest area of the cliff, gets steadily higher as the Central Rake rises. It has a number of ribs, which mark the lines taken by the main routes. The routes on the right of the buttress are some of the best on the cliff.

Saxifrage Rib 80 metres Very Difficult
A vague line that fails to reach the top of the cliff but provides relatively easy access to the Upper Central Cliff. Start at the foot of the ill-defined rib. Follow the rib direct on poor rock to the Central Rake.

Manchester Rib 81 metres Severe (9.4.50)
A much better way of gaining the Central Rake takes the prominent rib to the right. Start at a groove on the right-hand side of the rib.
1 30m. Climb the groove and its right wall to a stance level with the foot of a grass-filled cleft on the right, the Pis-Aller.
2 27m. Climb the rib by its right wall until easier climbing leads to a grassy ledge.
3 24m. Gain the detached block on the right and then get established on the main face. Continue up easier rock to the pinnacle at the top of the rib.

★Pis-Aller Rib 141 metres Severe (9.12)
A good route with a nice finish up an interesting arête, which is typical of the cliff. It takes the prominent rib in the centre of the cliff, which starts some 30 metres up. Start below the rib.
1 30m. Scramble up rock and vegetation to the terrace at the mouth of the Pis-Aller cleft (which the route sensibly avoids).
2 12m. Go rightwards across the steep wall to belay in a groove on the far edge.
3 27m. Follow ledges up to a wide crack. Climb the crack, and then move right into a groove on the edge of the rib. Ascend the groove to a grassy ledge.
4 24m. Climb up left of the rib to ledges and follow these up and rightwards to a belay on the edge.
5 24m. On poorer rock, climb over a pinnacle; then avoid the slab above by climbing the loose groove on the right, and follow the ridge to a stance.
6 24m. The ridge now falls back to a serrated knife-edge. Climb this and the rocks beyond to finish in the top of *Grass Pitch Gully*.

★Yellow Buttress 155 metres Severe (9.12)
One of the best routes on the cliff, taking a direct line up the buttress just left of Grass Pitch Gully. Start at the foot of the buttress below yet another rib.
1 30m. Scramble up mixed ground; then climb the cracked rib on the right to a ledge.
2 30m. Climb the obvious weakness in the slab above, with a move left to a ledge at 15 metres. Then go back right to follow the continuing line of weakness with interest to a grassy ledge. Continue up the rib to ledges overlooking the gully.
3 15m. Move left and climb the rib to the top of the main buttress.

4 34m. Regain the heathery ridge and climb it and the grassy groove on the left at times (a bit loose in places) to another stance overlooking the gully.
5 34m. Continue up to the pinnacles at the top of the buttress.
6 12m. Move left to join the preceding route and follow it to the top of *Grass Pitch Gully*.

Grass Pitch Gully   150 metres   Very Difficult   (1911)
The obvious gully to the right. A route that no longer lives up to its name. It gives two short pitches, then a long scramble to the site of the old grass pitch. Above this, easier climbing leads to a bay and an easy exit leftwards.

Lichen Ridge   135 metres   Very Difficult   (1911)
An interesting route with a fine gendarme, the usual amount of vegetation, and a little loose rock. Start at the foot of the ridge to the right of the gully.
1 30m. Ascend rock and heather to a steepening.
2 18m. Climb the left-hand side of the vegetated wall.
3 30m. Climb the arête above; then scramble to the foot of the gendarme.
4 12m. Climb the crack in the gendarme direct. It can be avoided on the left but this would be missing the point of the route somewhat.
5 27m. Continue along the ridge to belay below the final wall.
6 18m. Climb the wall on the right or, with more difficulty, on the left.

Avalanche Gully is the deep, loose gully bounding the right-hand side of the Central Cliff.

The Western Slabs

These are vegetated and unattractive, but being partially made up of rock they were climbed for King and Country back in a time when the crowds flocked to such cliffs as this.

Leo's Wall   120 metres   Very Difficult   (12.5.50)
A loose and vegetated route up the slabs just right of Avalanche Gully. Start by the foot of the gully and climb up trending rightwards to a heather terrace at 45 metres. Continue up the vegetation until the route steepens again, and then climb to the left of a shallow depression in the centre of the face to finish with another dose of heather and loose rock. A route for those desperately seeking solitude.

Approximately 100 metres right of Avalanche Gully is the obscure break of Civil Servant's Gully, which runs diagonally leftwards up the cliff. The foot of this can be reached direct over broken rock, but don't forget your umbrella!

Fox Route   64 metres   Very Difficult   (12.5.50)
The vegetated slabs right of Civil Servant's Gully. Start at the foot of the gully and climb first to the right, then to the left of the shallow groove in the slabs to a belay at 18 metres. Continue for another 18 metres until below a small tower. Traverse right across the slab below the tower until it is possible to gain the top of the tower. Scrambling remains.

About 30 metres right of the start of Civil Servant's Gully is the more obvious Raven Gully running directly up the cliff; this provides a reasonable descent from the routes hereabouts.

Oppenauer Slab 55 metres   Very Difficult   (12.5.50)
The large wet slab forming the left-hand side of Raven Gully. Start just left of the foot of the gully and climb the smooth slab direct to a belay about 5 metres below the steep edge of the red slab above. Climb diagonally rightwards to gain the slab and follow its right edge to the top. Mask and Snorkel recommended.

On the the steep right edge of Raven Gully is **Raven Buttress** (60 metres Very Severe) an unbalanced route with little difficulty apart from the mid-height bulge. Further right again, a desperate individual climbed **Dobbin** (50 metres Very Vegetated).

Craig Cwm Bychan   Small Cwm Crag   OS Ref 543 556

An area of much rock, which is unfortunately mostly wet and dirty. This, combined with the long approach, has deterred all but the most dedicated connoisseurs of the esoteric.

First, ascend to the summit of Mynydd Mawr and descend to the subsidiary summit of point 592, which overlooks Betws Garmon and the Castell Cidwm Hotel. From here, descend steep scree and broken ground for about 60 metres; then go diagonally right (facing out) to a small cairn before going back left (cairn). Descend a short gully on the left, which leads to the base of the crag.

Cities of Red Night 40 metres   Hard Very Severe 5a †   (8.00)
Meander at will up the blank wall/slab 6 metres left of *The Legend of Johnny Toto*, following the line of least resistance.

The Legend of Johnny Toto 46 metres   E2 5b †   (5.5.95)
An excellent route, but feasible in only the driest of conditions. Start in the middle of the crag, below an obvious stepped groove. Follow the groove to a short crack. Move out and continue directly up the red slab to cracks and a small overlap. Pull over and climb a crack to easier-angled rock which leads to the top. Belay well back on broken ground.

Castell Cidwm   Cidwm Castle   OS Ref 550 554

This large crag lies at the north-west end of Llyn Cwellyn, low down on the slopes of Mynydd Mawr. There is a lot of rock but much of it is broken by heathery ledges. By far the most significant climbing is concentrated on the South-East Face, overlooking the Afon Goch, which bounds the cliff to the left.

Castell Cidwm has undoubtedly the greatest concentration of harder routes of any crag in this area, some of which are of the highest quality. Despite a flurry of activity in the late 80s and the subsequent freeing of the roof above *Dwm*, new-route activity has fallen quiet and, at the time of writing, some of the cracks such as *Tramgo* are being overrun by ferns and trumpets. Considering the undoubted quality and difficulty of the routes, the cliff is somewhat neglected, giving connoisseurs the opportunity to climb in peace and solitude away from the madding crowd resident in the Pass on a summer weekend.

The South-East Face is very steep and presents few obvious features beyond an instant impression of serried overhangs. The rock is smooth, having an almost glassy texture, and generally very sound. The face takes no direct drainage but has a tendency to seep after heavy rain – particularly a problem on the last pitch of *Dwm*. The sunny aspect of the face quickly resolves this in good weather.

As the South-East Face is so featureless the following general indicators should help in locating the routes. Most start from the large grassy terrace, which is best gained at its left-hand end. The left-hand side of the face is dominated by a line of large overhangs, which are side-stepped by *The Curver* in a long rightward traverse. High in the smooth wall to the right of the overhangs is the prominent thin crack taken by the second pitch of *The Erg*, which reaches this point by a vague line up the wall below. Low in the centre of the face is a prominent V-groove used by *Central Wall*. Above this the face bulges out in a great prow – *Glwm*, after much wandering, finishes up the groove on its left. To the right again is the steep, shadowy corner of *Dwm*, capped by large overhangs. At this point the terrace at the base of the cliff turns uphill under the very steep walls and tiered overhangs through which *Tramgo* and *Hang 'em High* make their ways. One slight route (*Hors d'œuvre*) has been climbed on the buttress below and right of the main face.

The North-East Buttress of the cliff, lying to the right of the South-East Face, has produced a few routes of a mountaineering nature. Some poor routes have also been done on the small buttresses above the forestry track to Cidwm, on the south side of the Afon Goch. These have not been included and are left for the desperate to rediscover.

The normal approach to the cliff follows the forestry track above Llyn Cwellyn beginning at Planwydd (OS Ref 568 539), the farm on the Rhyd Ddu to Caernarfon road. This track reaches a disused quarry after about 15 minutes. Just after the quarry, the path leads up towards the crag by following the stream. This approach should not jeopardize access to this important cliff. Under no circumstances is an approach to be made from the Castell Cidwm Hotel across the end of the lake as this will upset the hotelier, Dŵr Cymru, the railway company, and last but not least the farmer. It is not so many years since he used climbers as target practice for his shot-gun. Safe parking at Planwydd is possible for a couple of cars owing to recent enlargement of the gateway. There is a proper car-park at the Snowdon Ranger youth hostel that is still free at the time of writing.

The best descent for the right-hand side of the South-East Face takes the slanting grassy rake below *Tramgo* and *Dwm*. For *Central Wall* and the other routes climbed from the gangway, it is possible to walk off right (facing out) and descend a grassy gully at the far end of the crag. Castell Cidwm Gully can be descended from routes on the North-East Buttress.

See pages 32a,b,c,d for diagrams.

Craig Planwydd OS Ref 552 552

In front of Castell Cidwm is a ridge running down the hillside between the forest and the Afon Goch. On the forest side of this ridge is a steep little crag of excellent rock similar to the parent crag. Approach as described above, but when the fence crosses the stream above the level of the top of the quarry, follow the fence between the ridge and the forest until the crag is reached after about 400 metres. It is steep and dark and has an undercut base. On the left-hand side is a gully which leads up to a steep wall and a corner.

Del Cap Corner 16 metres Hard Very Severe 5a † (21.4.03)
A well protected route that stays dry in the rain. Climb the right-trending corner to the bulging dark roof. Scuttle under this to the right and finish up a short chimney.

☆☆**Extreme Unction** 25 metres E3 6a † (21.4.03)
Excellent rock and protection (cams and wires), but a good pump. Left of centre of the steep wall is a short corner capped by a roof. Climb the corner and swing out right onto the wall. Climb direct up the wall on a variety of jugs and layaways to a distinct easing at half height. Step right and climb easier-angled rock to the top.

South-East Face

★**The Curver** 55 metres Hard Very Severe (26.9.60)
A good and popular route taking the easiest line on the face. It follows the obvious gangway under the overhangs on the left-hand side. Start in the corner below the start of the gangway under the large overhangs.
1 18m. 4c. Climb awkwardly onto the gangway and follow it rightwards to a niche. Peg belay.
2 37m. 4c. Traverse right again, moving round a steeper section, to continue on good holds in an airy situation. A more difficult move leads into a small finishing-corner. Rope-drag can be a problem on this pitch.

★★**Light Years** 37 metres E5 6b (5.6.88)
Wild, bold climbing through the middle of the big roofs above The Curver. The grade is the subject of some controversy, with opinions ranging from E4 6a to E6 6c! Start about 6 metres right of The Curver. Climb rightwards up a ramp; then slant back left to join The Curver at a smooth black slab. Climb to a small incut ledge directly above and continue to the crack beneath the roofs. Move left along the crack for 5 metres to a weakness in the roof. Powerful moves out and rightwards gain an undercut crack leading round into a corner. Climb the corner to the next roof and pull through rightwards to easy ground and belays above.

The Straighter 39 metres E2 (25.5.63)
A strenuous route, taking the easiest line up the steep wall below the traverse-line of *The Curver*. Thirty metres right of the corner at the start of *The Curver*, a smooth gangway leads upwards and rightwards above the terrace. Start at a large ledge half-way up the gangway where a shattered, blocky ramp-line runs back up and leftwards.
1 27m. 5b. From the top of the blocky ramp, climb the steep wall to a ledge-system. Go right for about 2 metres; then climb steeply up, trending leftwards to a prominent black hole beneath the overhangs. Move round the overhang on the left and climb up right to the bottomless chimney that leads to the traverse of *The Curver*; belay 3 metres to the left. Bold.
2 12m. 4c. Follow *The Curver* to the top.

★★The Erg 45 metres E5 (13.6.65)
This excellent steep route requires a considerably greater energy output than its name would imply. It takes a faint line of weakness right of *The Straighter* to reach the prominent crackline in the smooth wall right of the finish of *The Curver*.
1 27m. 5c. As for *The Straighter*, from the top of the blocky ramp, climb the steep wall to a ledge-system. Locate a prominent ramp 9 metres horizontally to the right and make a precarious unprotected traverse to reach its sanctuary (old peg). Pull onto the ramp past another peg and launch boldly onto the wall above. Climb the wall, first direct, then rightwards to a small stance (peg belay).
2 18m. 6b. Move up rightwards to beneath the daunting roof (pegs) and contort round the lip to a peg and good footholds; then follow the sustained seam direct, with a step left just below the top.

★★Equinox 37 metres E4 6a (22.10.88)
Good, varied climbing up the wall between *The Straighter* and *The Erg*. Take care with the rope drag. Start as for *The Straighter*. Climb straight up to a large pointed flake and continue direct to the traverse of *The Erg*. Move right a short way; then go up and left to some steep flakes leading up rightwards onto a slab. Trend leftwards up to the old slings and karabiners on *Cidwm Girdle*; then follow an obvious break diagonally left through the overhangs to gain the traverse of *The Curver*. Move up, then leftwards on flakes to finish.

★★★Potency 64 metres E6 (10.5.88)
A very steep and bold route that takes in the crux of *The Erg*. Not for the faint-hearted. Start from the terrace directly below the stance of *Central Wall*, at a good wire belay below a slabby wall undercut by a long roof.
1 27m. 6b. Climb the slabby wall and the short wall above; then move left past an ancient threaded tape and pull up left strenuously into a niche below a roof. Climb the wall above the niche, past a spike, to a shelf with good holds on the left (peg). Climb straight up above the peg to a line of holds leading leftwards to the stance of *The Erg*.
2 37m. 6b. Traverse right and pull through the roof as for *The Erg*; then follow the crackline for 8 metres to the flake where *The Erg* goes left. Step

Castell Cidwm 31

right and climb boldly up the middle of the face to good finishing-holds. Easier slabs lead to the top.

★★**Balance of Power**   61 metres   E5   (10.5.88)
An excellent, bold climb on perfect rock. It goes directly to the stance of *Central Wall* via an overhanging groove and then breaks left out of its second pitch. Start as for *Potency*.
1 24m. 6a. Climb straight up the middle of the slabby wall to a large block on a ledge. Go up the short wall above to a sloping ledge (peg). Move up and right with difficulty to a large sloping foothold; then step back left and climb to the base of the overhanging groove. Follow this, using a good crack on the left, to the stance of *Central Wall*.
2 37m. 5c. Climb up and go over the first set of overhangs as for *Central Wall*; then climb leftwards up the wall to an obvious good hold at the left-hand end of the roof. Pull round into a shallow groove, which leads to less steep rock. Bear left (still interesting) to the top.

★★★**Central Wall**   54 metres   E3   (3.10.64)
A classic, but some of the pegs are ancient and very rotten. Start in the middle of the grassy terrace below the obvious clean-cut V-groove.
1 24m. 5c. Reach the groove easily and follow it with difficulty to a tricky leftward exit at its top (peg) to gain a block. Climb the awkward wall above to reach the overhang (peg). Move up left to a good hidden hold and climb leftwards through the overhang (pegs) to gain a ledge (peg and nut belay).
2 30m. 5c. Move left for 2 metres; then climb diagonally back rightwards to the roof. Pull over on good holds and continue up a gangway to finish boldly leftwards through the capping roof.

★★★**Heading for Heights**   48 metres   E5   (27.5.88)
An excellent route, with a strenuous crux that breaches the great expanse of rock between *Central Wall* and *Vertigo*. Start as for *Vertigo*.
1 27m. 6b. Climb straight up the flake cracks above the belay until they end; then trend right up a ramp to join *Vertigo* at its crux. From the flake above, move up leftwards into a smooth open groove and follow this to a diagonal crack that leads up leftwards beneath a bulge. Move up on the left side of the bulge and use an undercut to make a long reach to a hidden slot in the wall above. Go up the wall to better holds in a groove, and follow this up and left to a nut belay below the steep white final wall.
2 21m. 5c. Move onto the wall and climb steeply up its left-hand arête to easier-angled rock. Keep right on the best line to the top.

★★**Vertigo**   39 metres   Hard Very Severe   (26.6.60)
A fine, steep, and exposed route on good holds, taking a diagonal line below the steepest section of the main face to an exposed finish above the dièdre of *Dwm*. Start at the extreme right-hand end of the terrace, some 6 metres right of the start of *Central Wall*, below and to the left of black slabs leading up to a scoop.
1 18m. 5a. Climb diagonally right for 6 metres to the left-hand end of the long overhang. Move left to out-flank it and go back right into the

scoop. Climb the scoop and exit right at the top (peg) to a good stance. Bold.

2 21m. 4c. Move rightwards round the arête to gain the obvious flaky crack and climb this steeply to the final bulges. Finish either up the small chimney above or, with maximum exposure and 'more charm', by traversing right until the top can be gained.

★**Glwm**   81 metres   E2   (27.9.64)

An exposed and tricky but wandering route that crosses the cliff searching for difficulties, which it finds in two otherwise unconnected pitches; the freeing of the original aided link pitch would give a much more impressive route of greater continuity. Start some 5 metres right of the start of *Vertigo*, where a small groove leads up to slabs and a prominent black roof.

1 24m. 5b. Climb up to the roof, and traverse right beneath it for 6 metres, until it is possible to break through at the obvious weakness. Climb up leftwards past a pinnacle to join and follow the first pitch of *Vertigo* rightwards to the stance.

2 30m. 5a. Move rightwards round the arête to gain the obvious flaky crack and climb this steeply to the final bulges, as for *Vertigo*; then traverse left to gain a stance in a corner.

3 12m. 5b. Move left to a spike and climb down to the lip of the overhangs beneath the prow. Move round the bulge on the left and climb up to a stance in the corner, below a steep green groove.

4 15m. 5a. Climb the groove to the top.

Variation

2a 30m. Using aid, follow the horizontal crack across the steep wall on the left of the stance. Go round the overhanging arête into a groove and pull over the roof to gain the stance.

Zwm   70 metres   E1 5b   (8.79)

Follow *Glwm* to the roof; then continue in a rightward-rising line to reach *Dwm* in the middle of its second pitch. Finish as for *Dwm*.

★★**Glasnost**   70 metres   E5   (5.6.88)

A long and sustained route, taking a leftward-trending line from the foot of *Dwm* to finish at the highest point of the crag near *Heading for Heights*. Start directly below the niche 6 metres up *Dwm*.

1 40m. 6a. Climb to the base of the niche; then hand-traverse left for 2 metres and pull up into a groove that is followed to some huge blocks. Step off the highest block, move up and right, and climb the steep wall to a resting-place below another steep section. Go up in the same line until forced left at some bulges (peg above on the girdle). Continue to join *Glwm*; then go more or less direct to the stance of *Vertigo*.

2 30m. 5c. From the right-hand side of the stance, climb straight up for 6 metres and then follow a break leftwards to a shallow groove leading to small ledges beneath the final wall. Climb the deep groove directly above to some steep finishing-moves, from which easier ground leads to a large thread belay at the top.

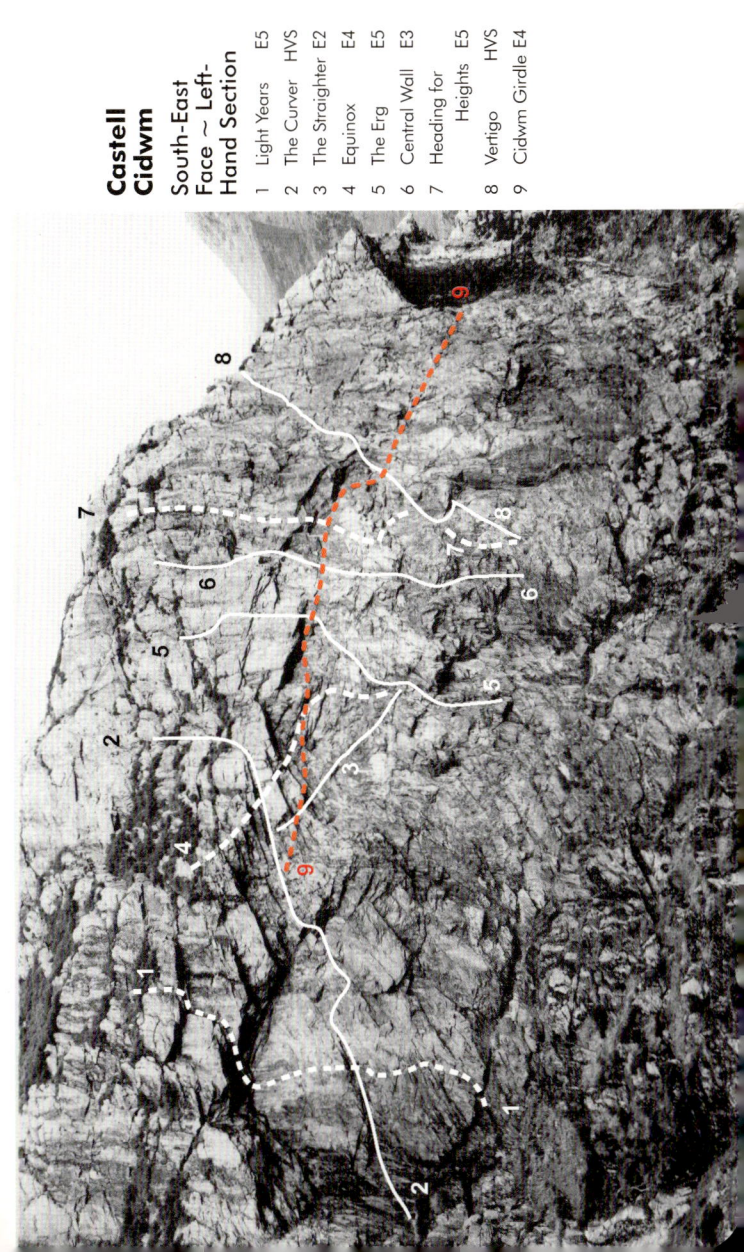

Castell Cidwm

South-East Face ~ Left-Hand Section

1. Light Years — E5
2. The Curver — HVS
3. The Straighter — E2
4. Equinox — E4
5. The Erg — E5
6. Central Wall — E3
7. Heading for Heights — E5
8. Vertigo — HVS
9. Cidwm Girdle — E4

Castell Cidwm

| 10 Dwmsday | E5 | 12 Dwm | E3 |
| 11 Freedwm Roof | E7 | 13 Tramgo | E4 |

14 Hang 'em High	E5
15 Howl at the Moon	E7
16 Walter Buffalo	E6

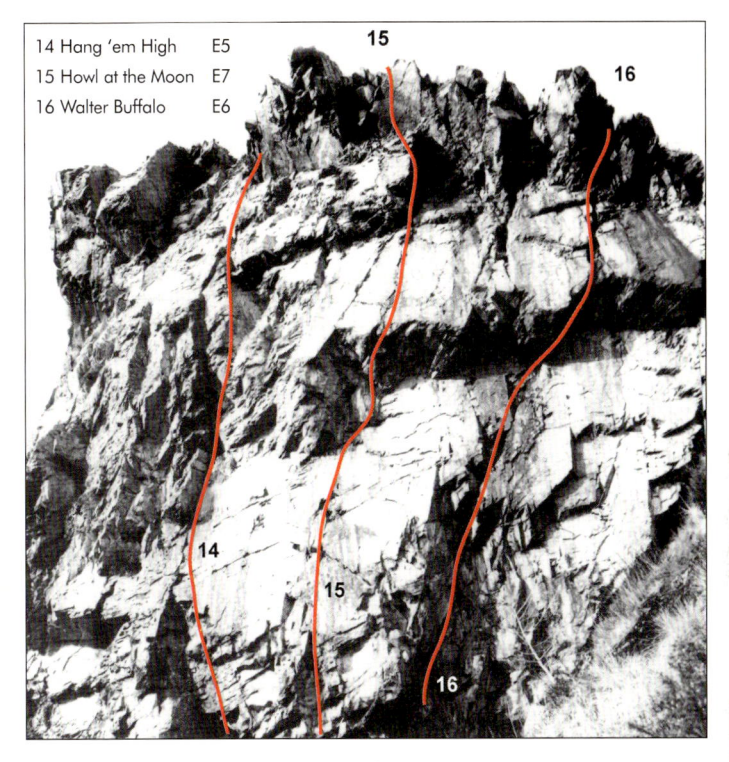

Dwmsday (E5), Castell Cidwm (first ascent, 1988)
Climber: Steve Monks   Photo: Pat Littlejohn

ACCESS TO CASTELL CIDWM

Approach from Planwydd ~ as there is no access from this end of Llyn Cwellyn

NORTH-EAST BUTTRESS

Castell Cidwm Gully

SOUTH-EAST FACE

Afon Goch

CRAIG PLANWYDD

Old Quarry

Private Land

Castell Cidwm 33

★★Dwmsday 51 metres E5 (4.6.88)

A forceful route taking the slim groove that cuts through the left side of the overhang above *Dwm*. Start as for *Dwm*.

1 21m. 6a. Climb into the niche and follow the crack up right for a short way before moving up left to a steep groove. Climb this and the easier wall above to a small stance at a cluster of three pegs.

2 30m. 6b. Move right to a peg (on *Dwm*); then climb more or less straight up the wall to a good crack beside a huge block beneath the overhang. Move up right into the groove and gain a sharp flake high on the left. Make a hard move into the rightward-slanting groove above the roof and follow this for 6 metres in a fine position to better holds leading up leftwards to the top of *Vertigo*.

★★Dwm 54 metres E3 (27.3.60)

A great route, the classic of the cliff, which follows the great overhung corner that is the most striking feature of the cliff. The final pitch is often wet and then usually requires some aid, but it gives excellent and unusual climbing when dry. Start on the grassy rake on the right-hand side of the cliff, below the great corner. A much better route when dry, when it can be done at about HVS if some aid points are used on the top pitch.

1 18m. 5a. Climb onto a large block and move left across the steep wall into a niche, or gain the niche direct with greater difficulty. Follow the crack rightwards out of the niche to reach a good ledge on the left.

2 18m. 5b. From the left-hand end of the ledge, climb the steep wall to another ledge. Admire the line of the girdle which goes out left; then, with difficulty, gain the wall on the right above the overhangs and teeter diagonally right to a tiny stance in the corner below the huge roof. Peg belays.

3 18m. 6a (or 4c+A1). Climb the corner-crack to the roof. Cursing the drainage, fight rightwards across beneath it (plenty of pegs) to gain a short chimney that leads quickly to the top. Alternatively, swing across to the chimney on aid. (Let's face it: if you pulled on the pegs you have cheated.)
Variation

Freedwm Roof E7 (27.6.96)

3a 27m. 6c. The hardest route in the guide. Follow pitch 3 to the roof; then gain the line of various pegs and other fixed gear. Climb the roof with the utmost difficulty. Very steep and very hard, definitely a test of ability in the horizontal plane.

★Tramgo 41 metres E4 6a (28.4.62)

This is the steep crackline of legendary strenuosity which splits the roofs right of *Dwm*. Unfortunately, the route was dirty before the 1989 guide was written and, as it has seen little traffic since, the ferns are taking over. An excellent route when clean. From below, the angle is deceptive: it is very steep. Much of the fixed gear is rotten; so, leaders, beware! Start further up the grassy rake from the corner of *Dwm*, at the foot of the crack. Move left across the wall to gain the crackline and follow it through two sets of overhangs. Climb the wall and groove above; then turn the next

★Hang 'em High   34 metres   E5 6a   (8.4.80)

The roof crack right of *Tramgo* is harder and more sustained than its partner. It is also very intimidating and makes one long for the vertical. Start 12 metres right of *Tramgo*, at a slightly higher level. Move up on good footholds and climb diagonally left past an old peg in a roof to another peg at a small ledge. Climb the crack above to a poor resting-place at a small niche. Steeper and more precarious moves lead up leftwards to a wide crack, where the angle eases. Finish easily.

★★Howl at the Moon   34 metres   E7 6c   (6.89)

This fierce route takes a direct line up the overhanging wall right of *Hang 'em High*, over the overlaps and the final roof, passing several pegs. Looks easy? It isn't! Both stamina and technique need to be spot on to succeed on Cidwm's answer to modern climbing.

☆☆Walter Buffalo   21 metres   E6 6a †   (5.93)

Just to the right is a vicious-looking forked crack. This route takes the right fork and is the epitome of a butch struggle. Climb past a groove to reach the crack. Struggle through the roof past a hanging fang with care into the off-width crack and subsequent roof. A route with good gear that requires plenty of brute force and determination.

★★★Cidwm Girdle   181 metres   E4   (10.65)

A superb trip, taking a high line across the cliff from right to left Although it never quite makes the top, the climbing is exposed and airy with great atmosphere. The pegs help with the route-finding, but most are ancient and do not necessarily offer secure protection!

1 18m. 5a. *Dwm* pitch 1.
2 27m. 5b. From the left-hand end of the ledge, climb the steep wall to another ledge. Follow the obvious leftward traverse for 5 metres to join *Glwm*. Pull through the overhang at the obvious weakness. Climb up leftwards past a pinnacle to join and follow the first pitch of *Vertigo* rightwards to the stance.
3 30m. 5a. *Glwm* pitch 2.
4 12m. 5b. *Glwm* pitch 3.
5 21m. 6a. Move left with difficulty and pull round into the final groove of *Central Wall* (peg). Reverse *Central Wall* to the belay ledge at the top of pitch 1.
6 9m. 5b. Move left round the arête and finger-traverse to a ledge beneath the roof, the second belay of *The Erg*.
7 27m. 6a. Semi-hand-traverse the crack that leads leftwards across the wall to a spike, and continue with difficulty by blind moves to a niche in the roofs. Descend very steeply for 5 metres to a slab, and follow it to a junction with *The Straighter*. Climb steeply up leftwards to a prominent black hole beneath the overhangs. Move round the overhang on the left

and climb up and right to the bottomless chimney which leads to the traverse of *The Curver*. Belay 3 metres to the left.
8 37m. 4c. Descend the leftward-sloping gangway to the grassy bay on the left of the cliff (pitch 1 of *The Curver* in reverse).

Hors d'œuvre   69 metres   Very Severe   (28.4.62)
A scrappy route taking the obvious groove-lines in the more broken area of rock below and to the right of the main face. Not really what most people come here for. Start in the middle of the lower wall by a red slab below an obvious open groove.
1 30m Climb a short wall right of the slab to a grassy ledge. Step left and climb the groove. Move left through a holly to gain a stance.
2 15m. Follow grass up leftwards to a stance below a groove.
3 24m. Make a descending traverse rightwards for 9 metres to gain the central groove and follow it to a small ledge. Move right awkwardly to another ledge and continue to the top.

North-East Buttress

The buttress is bounded by the easy Castell Cidwm Gully, which contains one wet cave pitch of 5 metres. The first climb takes the wall overlooking the gully on the right.

Finale Wall   66 metres   Very Difficult   (25.6.50)
A poor route. Start at the narrowing of Castell Cidwm Gully, some 30 metres above the cave pitch.
1 9m. From a metre or so up the right wall, ascend broken rock to a belay on the right edge of the gully.
2 18m. Climb the wall above to the left-hand end of a heather ledge.
3 15m. Climb the bulge above and continue up cracks to a narrow ledge.
4 24m. Move round to the left of an overhang and continue more easily to the top.

Wolf's Buttress   120 metres   Difficult   (1905)
A vague climb, taking the easiest line up the buttress. Start about 10 metres below the narrow entrance to Castell Cidwm Gully. Scramble steeply up to the foot of a heathery slab. Climb the slabs for 45 metres to a large grassy bay beneath an overhang. Escape leftwards and continue up for some 30 metres to the right-hand of two conspicuous chimneys splitting the upper part of the cliff. Tree belay. Climb the chimney in two pitches to the top.
Variation   50 metres   Very Difficult
From the tree belay, trend left over loose, vegetated rock to climb a steep striated wall, and belay on the ledge above. Follow the ledge up to the right, and climb a steep crack to easy ground.

Lamb's Leap   111 metres   Severe   (9.4.50)
A route that seeks out harder pitches on the main buttress but still manages to get its share of the vegetation. Start in the grassy bay above the first section of *Wolf's Buttress*.

1 24m. Climb the loose and awkward right-hand corner of the overhang and continue rightwards up the vegetated wall above to a stance.
2 24m. Go up the steepening slabs, moving leftwards near the top.
3 12m. Traverse 5 metres right and climb the steep corner to belay on the right of a rowan tree.
4 15m. Climb the small overhang and continue delicately to a narrow ledge.
5 18m. Continue straight up to a grassy terrace, and belay at the foot of the final slabs.
6 18m. Start up the crack and finish steeply on good holds.

To the right of Castell Cidwm Gully a shallow gully-line divides the buttress; the next two routes take the clean rock to its right.

The Mystery II   116 metres   Hard Severe
This route had been cleaned and presumably climbed by an unknown party prior to the first recorded ascent. Start on a grassy ledge, above the left-hand end of a small stone-walled enclosure, with a pile of blocks at its right-hand end. It is reached by scrambling up to the right of a tree.

1 37m. 4a. From the left-hand end of the ledge, go awkwardly up to the left and move up over ledges to a groove-line. Follow a crack up the groove, passing a ledge and tree at 20 metres, to reach a slab. Belay behind a bollard.
2 15m. Go easily up the slab to belay near the bottom of a rake.
3 18m. Gain the wall behind the belay and continue up rightwards on small holds to a horizontal crack. Traverse right to belay on a block ledge.
4 46m. Reverse the traverse and climb a groove to an overhang. Turn this on the left using dubious blocks, and continue steeply up shattered rock to reach easier-angled slabs. Pleasant climbing leads to the top.

Acrophily   115 metres   Very Severe   (23.4.72)
An open line generally to the right of *Mystery II*, with a delectable finish on the upper buttress. Start on the same ledge as that route.

1 15m. 4c. From the blocks at the right-hand end of the ledge, step up left and climb a steep groove to a small square overhang. Turn this on the right by a difficult move and continue to a cave with a tree belay on the right.
2 40m. 4c. Step left from the cave and go up to a ledge on the left. Continue direct to a niche and step right to climb a steep and undercut mossy groove. Finish left with difficulty to reach the bollard belay of the preceding route.
3 15m. Go easily up the slab to the rake; then walk a further 15 metres up the rake to belay beneath a rightward-slanting ramp.
4 30m. 4b. Gain the ramp from the right and move up it past a dubious block; then go up a short wall to the right on good holds to a niche. Step

down and left from the niche and climb a steep crack to a small ledge. Move up leftwards on small holds in an exposed position to reach a flake hold below the final bulge. Step left again and move up to a small ledge above the line of overhangs. Belay a metre higher.
5 15m. Finish easily up slabs.

Llechog Slabby   OS Ref 597 537

Llechog is the large cliff bounding the southern rim of Cwm Clogwyn beneath the ridge taken by the Snowdon track from Beddgelert and Rhyd Ddu. It provides plenty of interesting climbing in fine mountain situations.

The cliff faces north-east, but in the middle of summer receives plentiful sunshine until early afternoon. About 120 metres high, it is set at high slab angle and takes little drainage, which provides a welcome contrast with many of the crags in this area. The quality of the rock is variable but on the best routes it is sound, rough, and so compact that protection can be difficult to find.

Two distinct approaches to the crag are possible. The first is to park in the National Park car-park in Rhyd Ddu (pay and display – £2 per day at the time of writing) and follow the Snowdon path, which leads to the top of the cliff within an hour. There is a grassy ramp 300 metres down to the left, taking you easily to the base of the crag. It is also possible to descend the Central Couloir but this is loose and unpleasant. The alternative and generally preferred approach, though longer, is to park at the Snowdon Ranger Youth Hostel, follow the Snowdon Ranger path almost to Bwlch Cwm Brwynog, and contour rightwards round towards the crag. This is certainly the best way to Llechog Facet. It has the advantage of free parking and allows you to see the crags as you approach. It may, however, be a little boggy.

The cliff is divided into two sections by the Central Couloir. The best of the climbing lies on the steeper section right of this couloir, the Western Cliff. The Eastern Cliff is easier-angled and more broken, trailing off to the left into scree. Distinctive features of the Eastern Cliff include the long narrow *Arrow Slab* high up to the left, and the steeper quartzy area taken by *Central Rib*.

The first feature of the Western Cliff, to the right of the Central Couloir, is a typical gutter, Mermaid Gully, which runs to slightly more than half the height of the cliff. A slabby area right of its base gives the start of *The Mermaid Climb*, which traverses rightwards across the terrace above to finish up a depression on the left of a prominent red slab.

The three-tiered buttress capped by the red slab is taken by *Resurrection*. Right again are vegetated slabs capped by a dark diagonal rock cornice. *The Cloister Climb* runs up to the left-hand side of this. *Black Rib*, clearly visible from the right but not the left, ascends to the lower end of the cornice and is bounded on the right by Central Gully.

Immediately right of the gully is *Central Ridge*, which bounds Trinity Buttress A on the left. *Five Cave Gully*, conspicuous by its cluster of four caves near the top, separates Trinity Buttresses A and B. *Blood on the Tracks* takes the left edge of Trinity Buttress B. To the right again is Grey Gully, then Trinity Buttress C with its obvious smooth lower wall taken centrally by *Slopey*. The climbing is bounded to the right by the deep cleft of *The North Gully*.

The Central Couloir provides an unpleasant descent from all of the routes. The top of this can be recognized as a depression some 20 metres left of a stone wall (facing outwards) crossed by the Snowdon path. Descend into the couloir via a left-hand branch (facing outwards), which begins slightly to the left of the main depression. If you want the safer option, walk 300 metres along the top of the cliff towards the north-west and descend the grassy ramp. This is easier but care is still necessary.

See page 48a for diagram.

Eastern Cliff

Arrow Slab 118 metres Very Severe (6.7.55)
On the left side of the Eastern Cliff is the striking *Arrow Slab*, which climbs the upper slab. Start at the back of a slight bay some 50 metres left of *Central Rib*. Arrows and the name may be discerned faintly scratched on the slab above the cairn.
1 18m. 4b. Climb up the slab for 8 metres. Traverse right beneath grooves and ascend the rightmost one. Step left awkwardly after 6 metres to a poor stance in a niche.
2 17m. Traverse 3 metres right from the niche and climb ribbed rock to a small overhang. Trend left to a grassy ledge beneath a slab.
3 35m. Continue up the slabs for about 30 metres, crossing a grassy rake; then move left to a recess.
4 18m. Climb diagonally right over ribs.
5 30m. Continue to the top.

The next three routes take the slab below the Arrow Slab, and finish at a spike that makes a convenient abseil anchor.

Strange Fruit 40 metres E1 5b (28.8.01)
A worthwhile route up the left-hand side of the slab. Start at the base and take a thin crack up leftwards to an obvious narrow quartz band. Move up a shallow groove-system to the left edge of the slab. Step back right and continue direct to reach the left end of a grassy slanting crack.
Hand-traverse this rightwards to reach good gear-slots and take the leftward-slanting fault to finish. Scramble up right to the abseil spike.

★★**The Pickpocket** 40 metres E2 5c (28.8.01)
Good climbing up the centre of the slab to a thought-provoking finish. Start at the base of the slab and climb direct for 9 metres to reach a fragile flake. Continue up and slightly right to reach the obvious triangular niche in the middle of the slab. From here, climb diagonally right; then swing left

☆**While the Cat's Away** 40 metres E2 5c † (23.9.01)
Start to the right of the preceding route, below a short grassy groove.
Climb up left of the groove and gain a small grass ledge a metre or so
below its top. Traverse right; then go up to a cluster of pockets. Move up a
metre and then trend right to the diagonal break. Cross this using good
holds, and continue to the spike.

To the right is a slab with a prominent hanging arête.

Gambit 37 metres Hard Very Severe 5a (23.6.01)
Start beneath the slab. Pull up grass to reach the slab, and trend
rightwards to gain a block. Traverse left to the arête and continue up,
passing an overhang on the right, to reach a ledge and a block belay.
Abseil off.

Below *Arrow Slab* is a 15-metre rocky bluff emerging from the scree. The
diagonal cracks on the right have been climbed at Severe, while the obvious
line just left of the nose has an unprotected 5c move at 8 metres.

★**Central Rib** 123 metres Very Difficult (1911)
A good slab route. A prominent left-slanting rib high up in the centre of the
cliff gives the climb its name. Start at the lowest point reached by the Eastern
Cliff, in a little bay 20 metres left of a prominent quartz-speckled toe.
1 30m. Pleasant slab climbing 'with good holds economically supplied.
Also useful are sundry little round cavities into which the digits of a limb
can be fitted to a nicety'.
2 27m. Easier slabs lead to a series of grassy terraces.
3 12m. Climb a crack to a pinnacle above and to the right. The main rib
rises from a grassy terrace 6 metres to the right.
4 30m. Climb the rib direct on small holds near its left edge to a ledge
and small belay on the right.
5 24m. Continue easily past a quartz-spattered bay to the top.

An unidentifiable route, **Cross Slab and Arête** (100 metres Very Difficult
6.7.55), has been climbed between *Central Rib* and the next route.

From near the foot of the Central Couloir, a continuous narrow gutter,
Eastern Gutter, runs nearly to the top of the cliff. The slabs on its left are
conspicuously marked with black.

Torpedo Route 105 metres Difficult (18.6.11)
This route follows the slab on the left of the gutter. Easy climbing on sound
rock, the holds 'a source of quiet delight', leads up the slabs for 60 metres
to a grass terrace. The ribbed wall above is climbed with some interest.
The difficulty gradually eases after a steeper grooved section has been
passed. Continue easily to the ridge.

Eastern Gutter 85 metres   Very Severe (9.11)
A mysterious, and for many years lost, route: one of the earliest of its grade in Wales, and one of the more interesting lines on the Eastern Cliff.
1 18m. Typical gully-climbing until the bed steepens and becomes a groove curving up to the left. Poor belay.
2 30m. 4c. The groove gives sustained bridging increasing in difficulty to grassy ledges at 18 metres. Scramble up to belay.
3 37m. Continue up typical Llechog slabs and grass to the top.

The huge Central Couloir contains one pitch of Difficult standard – a slabby chimney-groove of 12 metres on loose rock, high up in the main branch.

Western Cliff

The area of rock immediately to the right of the Central Couloir is very broken and the rock is poor towards the top. The next route lies to the right of another characteristic gutter, Mermaid Gully.

The Mermaid Climb 107 metres   Severe (1911)
On the right of Mermaid Gully is an area of slabby ribs leading up to a heathery terrace. Start at the foot of these ribs.
1 34m. Climb the steep slabby ribs, keeping to the right. Continue up slabs to the terrace.
2 34m. Traverse the terrace and go up easy rock to the base of a V-groove.
3 18m. Climb the smooth groove with difficulty to a stance.
4 21m. Continue up beside the red slab of *Resurrection* into a chimney on the left. Climb this to gain easier rock and thence the top.

To the right, a prominent buttress composed of three tiers of slabs provides the best climbing on the cliff.

★The Circus Animals' Desertion 115 metres   E2 (21.8.94)
A direct line up the left-hand side of the *Resurrection* slabs.
1 24m. *Resurrection* pitch 1.
2 24m. 5b. Climb an overlap and move left to a thin crack leading to a ledge. Another thin crack leads to a large ledge, from which a left-facing corner is followed.
3 30m. Climb the crack up the left-hand side of the next wall to a horizontal break. Continue up and left to a spike, and descend to belay in the groove.
4 37m. 5b. Climb the curving crack on the arête to a ledge at the foot of a groove. Follow the crack to a junction with *Resurrection*, which provides the finish.

★Resurrection 124 metres   Hard Very Severe (15.8.70)
This fine near-classic route takes a direct line up the three smooth slabs of the buttress, the top slab being the 'gaunt red crag' – described as 'quite impossible' by Archer Thomson. Although it is possible to escape between pitches this does not detract from the climbing, which increases

progressively in difficulty and quality. Start directly below the lower tier of the buttress, 10 metres left of the shallow gully of the start of *The Cloister Climb*.
1 24m. Scramble up heathery breaks to belay at the foot of the first wall.
2 30m. 4a. Move into the gully on the right and climb it easily for a short way (junction with *Zarquon*). Traverse left across some perched blocks; then continue straight up into a shallow groove. Climb this and the short crack above to a large grassy ledge. Belay on the right.
3 30m. 4c. Climb the edge of the slab to gain and follow a short right-facing groove to a ledge on the left. Continue delicately up the open groove on the left into a shallow scoop. Step left round the rib and move up to easier climbing, which leads to a belay in a minor gully on the left.
4 40m. 5a. Climb directly up the crack in the centre of the smooth final slab until a thin diagonal crack can be followed to the left-hand edge of the slab. Swing round the arête and cross the steep wall to gain a corner. Move left again and follow a crack over a bulge to a small ledge. Move back right across the groove onto the front face and climb to the top.
Variations

★**Erection** E2 (24.7.82)
4a 30m. 5c. The proper way up the 'gaunt red crag': a fine pitch, taking the line that the original should have done. Follow pitch 4 to the left arête and climb the thin crack just right of the edge to the top.

☆**Hellraiser** E1 † (27.6.93)
4b 30m. 5b. The right-hand side of the 'gaunt red crag'. From the bottom right-hand side of the slab, take the obvious stepped footholds diagonally left and make some awkward moves up to a small grassy ledge. Continue up the cracks to the top.

The best combination hereabouts is to start up *Zarquon*, join *Resurrection*, and then finish up *Erection*. This gives a ★★ outing.

The Cloister Climb 108 metres Severe (18.6.11)
An interesting route up the vegetated slabs below the huge diagonal rock cornice, but rather spoilt by the vegetation. Start in the shallow gully right of *Resurrection*, to the right of the heathery area beneath the red slab.
1 27m. Climb easily up the groove for 10 metres; then take a right-hand branch until a traverse right leads to the edge and a grassy ledge.
2 24m. Step right and move up onto the main slab. Climb the slab, trending slightly left to a stance.
3 27m. Continue up the slabs in the same line, move left, and go up a groove to another large grassy ledge.
4 30m. Climb a slim groove in the centre of the main slab into a recess – The Cloister – under the cornice. Traverse left until a rough chimney leads suddenly to the top.

Zarquon 102 metres E1 (14.8.82)
A natural line up the left-hand edge of the slabs right of *Resurrection*, which crosses, then finishes up, *The Cloister Climb*. The first two pitches

give a good alternative start for *Resurrection* or *Erection*. Start up to the right from the foot of the edge, in a bay left of a pillar.
1 18m. 5a. Go straight up thin cracks to the grassy ledge at the top of pitch 1 of *The Cloister Climb*.
2 15m. 5a. Climb diagonally left across the pink slab into a recess. Continue leftwards up a groove to a stance right of the blocks on pitch 2 of *Resurrection* (which can be joined at this point). A bold pitch.
3 21m. 4b. Climb the corner-crack and the slab above to a heathery ledge.
4 18m. Climb up right to a crack and groove, which are followed to another large ledge on *The Cloister Climb*.
5 30m. *The Cloister Climb* pitch 4.

Black Rib   80 metres   Difficult   (18.6.11)
A pleasant route, taking the dark-coloured rib, so obvious from the right, which runs up to the right of the lower end of the cornice. The rock is of a texture different from that of the rest of the cliff – steep and with plenty of holds. Start at the foot of the rib.
1 46m. Climb the rib past possible stances to belay in a large bay.
2 34m. Climb the rightmost of the three ribs rising from Central Gully on the right, starting from a recess on its left side and moving onto the edge, which is followed to the top. Other lines have also been climbed.

To the right is Central Gully, the right-hand rib of which gives:

Central Ridge   120 metres   Difficult   (1911)
A pleasant climb on excellent rock. Intermediate belays are available. Start on the right near the foot of Central Gully. Gain the crest of the rib and follow it for 60 metres to a grassy platform. From a grassy chimney to the right, traverse left to gain the edge again and follow it to another ledge. Pass a small overhang on the left and continue to the top.

☆☆**Y Bwbach Llwyd**   43 metres   E2 5b †   (17.6.00)
Good climbing on perfect rock. Start in a recessed grassy bay up and right of the foot of *Central Ridge*. Move up left to gain the arête and continue to a poor spike runner in a large pocket. A hard move leads to some scoops and a good nut. Move back right onto the rib above some grass. Continue up the central runnel and a final steep wall to join *Central Ridge*. Spike belay. Abseil off or follow the ridge to the top.

Trinity Buttress A to the right has an unmistakable square-cut overhang at its base.

☆**Diwrnod I'r Brenin**   46 metres   E2 6a †   (22.7.00)
Climb the dirty slab at the right-hand side of the overhang until a hard move left gains the slab and a good hold. Delicately climb the slab to the top. Climb the steep wall above (good wires), and move left to reach easy grooves, which lead to a large grass ledge and thread belay. Abseil off.

☆Lliwedd Comes to Llechog 48 metres E2 5b † (13.5.00)
Start up the clean rib to the right and reach some obvious flakes. Move up and left to a sloping ledge (spike); then make hard moves up the slab to better holds. Climb up, trending right and then back left to a vegetated ledge (*Friend* 2½ belay possible). Pull back right onto the slab and continue up and right to better holds. Climb the groove above to a good hold where the angle steepens. Continue up the groove to a grass ledge. Spike belay above. Abseil off.

★★Plant y Fflam 46 metres E2 5b (13.5.00)
Another good pitch on excellent rock, which takes the hidden hanging slab just right of the preceding route and left of *Five Cave Gully*. Climb a slabby wall to a large ledge. Move up right of an overhang to gain the obvious scooped central groove. Follow this to a bulge and continue to gain another scoop, which leads into a corner. Pull leftwards onto the centre of the slab, and climb up past a good pocket to the top. Abseil off.

A Taste of Honey 46 metres Hard Very Severe 5a (13.5.00)
The obvious rib, which is gained from the left-hand side. Continue directly up the rib to reach a grassy ledge. Climb the shallow corner, and move up and left to reach a dirty corner. An awkward move up leads to grassy ledges. Abseil off.

Five Cave Gully 116 metres Hard Severe (1911)
The conspicuous gully with prominent caves. Start at the foot of the gully.
1 40m. Climb the bed of the gully to the first cave at 25 metres. Step left to a grassy ledge and climb the groove above to another groove, which leads to a heather terrace.
2 46m. Scramble up the gully bed to the four caves above.
3 30m. 4a. Start up the left wall of the first of the four, and then move right. Climb the second cave direct and evade the final two on the left.

Between *Five Cave Gully* and *Grey Gully* is Trinity Buttress B.

☆☆After the Goldrush 46 metres E3 5c † (26.6.01)
This route takes the prominent crackline on the left side of Trinity Buttress B. Start immediately right of *Five Cave Gully*. Climb the clean rib up to a corner, and step left to a small ledge beneath the crack. Follow the crack with sustained interest to reach the left edge of the ledge (also visited by *Blood on the Tracks*). A tricky move up left leads to a leaning corner. Bridge up and pull out left at the top. Move up to a large block belay. Abseil off.

★Blood on the Tracks 106 metres E1 (29.5.78)
A good natural line up the nose of the buttress, giving some fine and bold delicate climbing. It is possible to abseil off after the first two pitches. Start at the foot of an obvious rib at the lowest part of the buttress.
1 34m. 5b. Go straight up the rib by shallow grooves, and follow the single groove, which breaks through the smoothest and steepest section to ledges on the left. Continue up a final short groove to a large grassy ledge on the right.

2 15m. 5a. Follow the central groove through the bulge above; then move left and go steeply up a rib to more ledges.
3 30m. Ascend easy ground to the final wall. An unpleasant scramble.
4 27m. 4b. Gain the ochre-coloured scoop slightly left of centre, and follow it to easy ground and the top.

The vegetated central area of this buttress has been climbed by various routes. All of these take only vague lines with much scope for variation.

Sunset Slabs 115 metres Severe (9.56)
Start in the middle of the buttress. Climb slabs for 30 metres to a vegetated ledge. Traverse left to the base of another area of slab, and climb this to more heather (25 metres). Ascend a short steep wall to trees. Climb the wall on the left, with difficulty at first, to reach a stance in a grassy chimney. Follow chimneys and cracks to the ridge.

Trinity Buttress B 70 metres Severe (9.11)
Another vague climb, starting just left of *Grey Gully and Wall*, takes an indeterminate line to the top of the cliff. Begin at the foot of two slimy ribs. Climb either rib and step left into a groove. Then go up vegetation to a terrace below an overhang (20 metres). Avoid this on the right and follow a rib to a ledge. From its right-hand end, follow a shallow groove bearing left to easier ground (30 metres). Climb the upper wall – hard if taken direct, but avoidable by a grassy chimney to the left. Start the steep wall above direct; then traverse to the right and finish up another shallow grassy chimney.

Grey Gully and Wall 90 metres Severe (1911)
Vegetated gully-climbing leads to a fine finish.
1 27m. Climb the gully bed and vegetation on its right to a ledge.
2 21m. Continue up the gully to a large heathery ledge below the final wall.
3 27m. Climb the shallow depression in the wall, to the left of the grassy chimney line, to reach a ledge.
4 15m. Continue easily in the same line to the top.

The buttress to the right is Trinity Buttress C, which has an impressive smooth lower section taken by *Slopey* and three more recent routes.

Trinity Buttress C 79 metres Severe (1913)
The left-hand side of the buttress is split by a series of grooves. Start at a conspicuous leaning block 10 metres from the lowest point of the buttress.
1 21m. Climb the groove to a scoop above a grassy ledge. From a higher ledge, traverse right to a steep slanting groove and go up over grassy ledges to a flat, balanced block.
2 23m. Climb the wall above to a heathery ledge. Follow an awkward groove to easier climbing leading up to a steep wall.
3 23m. Climb the wall, trending left, and traverse right to a small ledge. Ascend a steep corner to its right on small holds.

4 12m. Follow the arête above on its right edge to finish up a short crack in the face.

Slopey starts below the main slab of the buttress, on the narrow ledge at the top of pitch 1 of *Slab and Groove*. The first two routes begin on a grassy ledge just to its left at a slightly higher level.

Skirmish   43 metres   Hard Very Severe   5a   (22.7.00)
Step right from the right-hand end of the grassy ledge to reach a hidden crack. Climb the crack for a short way and move left into a groove. When the groove steepens, go diagonally right to an indefinite arête. Climb the arête, using the left-hand side to reach easier ground and a spike. Abseil off.

The Man Who Shot a Fox   43 metres   E3 5c †   (22.7.00)
A controversial route because the peg placed for this route can be clipped from *Slopey*, sanitizing that route somewhat. Perhaps it would be best if it were removed? Start as for *Skirmish*, but climb the crack to its top at a horizontal break (peg on the right). Keeping left of the peg, go up the slab to a ledge on the left (sustained and bold). Traverse a metre right into the groove of *Slopey*, and climb this and easier ground above to reach the abseil spike.

★★**Slopey**   30 metres   E3 5c   (2.8.81)
This sustained and precarious pitch follows the obvious break slanting leftwards up the wall. Climb the left-hand of the twin central cracks for about 12 metres to a horizontal break where the crack ends. Then step up right and climb the right-hand of the cracks. Continue up and slightly right to a horizontal crack near the top, step back left, and climb a short smooth groove and easier ground above to finish on the terrace. Abseil off.

Future Tense   46 metres   E1 5b   (22.7.00)
Right of *Slopey* is a crack-system running up the slab to join the arête defining the right-hand side of the buttress. Climb the cracks to the arête and continue up this for a metre or so. Follow the leftward crackline above to reach the groove on *Slopey*. Climb the groove to easier ground. Abseil off.

Slab and Groove   114 metres   Very Severe   (17.9.49)
Start at the foot of the buttress, almost in *The North Gully*.
1 15m. Climb the groove on the right to a grassy ledge.
2 30m. Go up to a crack near the right-hand edge of the slab and follow this for 20 metres until a traverse left is possible along a slanting crack to gain the top of the slab.
3 30m. Scramble up heather to a rib overlooking *The North Gully*.
4 12m. Climb the groove until it becomes difficult; then continue up flakes on its left edge.
5 27m. Climb the steep wall above.

The North Gully (Very Difficult 1911) gives broken climbing with two pitches: an 18-metre groove low down and a 5-metre chimney. The rest is rather loose scrambling, with climbing available as desired.

Llechog Facet
OS Ref 592 545

This is the line of four small cliffs which lie below the rim of Cwm Clogwyn. They are of interest only when the hills have been dry for some time, being small, north-facing, vegetated, and usually wet. The Afon Treweunydd flowing from Llyn Nadroedd cascades between the Far North Bluff and the North Bluff. A stone wall descends from the South Bluff to join the wall dividing the cliff from the marshy area in the valley bottom. A scruffy bluff exists between the North and South Bluffs but, like the Far North, has no routes. Approach from the Snowdon Ranger Youth Hostel, as for Llechog.

See page 48d for diagram.

North Bluff

This, the largest of the four cliffs, displays a dual personality. The left-hand side is slabby and vegetated, and the routes, beneath a sloping grass terrace, are scarcely worth recording. **Batelion** (40 metres Severe) starts at the foot of the slabby area, climbs the slab to grass, and then continues to the top. About 12 metres right of this, **The Bar Steward** (37 metres Very Difficult 25.7.50) starts off a rocky table and ascends a shallow ridge to finish up the wall above. **The Greenhouse Roof** (60 metres Very Difficult 9.6.51) starts about 30 metres above and to the right of *The Bar Steward* and takes a vague ridge through vegetation and wanders on to the top. **Nadroedd** (90 metres Severe 18.9.49) ascends the heathery buttress bounding the North Bluff on the right.

However, wedged between *The Bar Steward* and *The Greenhouse Roof* is a steep section of cliff, curiously rather light in colour, bristling with overhangs, which promises climbing of an entirely different character.

Chantilly Lace   30 metres   E2   5c   †   (1.9.96)
A fine introduction to the style of climbing here. Start over to the left beneath twin cracks that form a flat pillar. Climb straight up the initial groove and right-hand crack. Slip to the left at the bulge and into a vertical slot. Climb the slot to the headwall and finish in style: swing boldly rightwards along a horizontal flake in the upper wall and climb a sharp crack.

☆**Another Green World**   34 metres   E3   6a   †   (1.9.96)
The big capped corner in the centre looks a simple affair, but a snare lies in the tangle of overhangs above. Climb steeply up to the corner. After some solid jamming and bridging, sneak round the edge to bypass the huge overhang. There is no easy escape. Make a sensational diagonal traverse rightwards to the peg on *Good Golly Miss Molly*. Climb over the very difficult overlap and then step back left across a groove to reach a steep crack in the headwall.

☆☆**Good Golly Miss Molly**   27 metres   E4   6a   †   (16.8.95)
Part way up the cliff, a slender, eye-catching groove just demands attention. Strength and subtlety are prerequisites as this route is very steep indeed! Start

on a narrow ledge above the substrata. Climb a little open corner and then up the leaning groove. A hard move right leads up into the apex of a bottomless cranny. Pull blindly out left to a cramped perch. Now move up to a peg and through the final difficult overlap, where a sidle rightwards on a good chicken-head leads round onto an edge and the top.

☆**Shake, Rattle, and Roll**   27 metres   E4 6a †   (16.8.95)
An intricate linking of features makes another very good climb. Start from the same ledge as, but right of, *Good Golly Miss Molly*. An oblong overhang soon blocks a short corner, so take the slanting crack to an overhung niche on the right. Bridge out of this and, with a lusty pull, straddle a nose. Now tackle the crack and make a very mean stride right at its top to a more reasonable finishing-groove.

Lazing on a Sunny Afternoon   27 metres   E1 5b †   (10.8.97)
A good corner-crack defines the right-hand end of the face. Scramble to its base; then bridge, jam, and layback all the way. Well protected and a sheer delight.

South Bluff

This provides only three routes.

Residents' Wall   34 metres   Very Severe   (24.2.49)
The route follows the obvious overhanging flake crack. Start 6 metres right of the stone wall and climb a ramp to an overhang, which is avoided by a short crack on the left. Then go back right and belay below the flake. Climb the difficult overhanging crack. Continue easily up the crack to the top of the flake and finish delicately up the wall above.

Summer Buttress   39 metres   E4 †   (12.6.98)
To the right of *Residents' Wall* is an obvious drainage line with a brown buttress to the right. The route takes the crest of this buttress and gives steep and sustained climbing. Start at the subsidiary rib right of the drainage.
1 18m. 5b. Climb a slabby rib; then go left over heather to belay beneath a short steep corner.
2 21m. 6a. Climb the corner past a bulge on the left; then trend back right. Break left again through a second bulge to gain a resting-place. Move right and climb a thin crack and short groove to a ledge below the final arête, which gives an exciting finish.

The Little Rocker   43 metres   Very Severe   (19.3.66)
Start at the lowest point of the cliff.
1 9m. Climb the wall to a terrace.
2 34m. Follow a wide slabby groove for 8 metres until forced right onto the rib. Climb the groove above and gain a good ledge on the left. Move up leftwards for a short way, surmount a block, and go left to climb the crack to the top.

Carreg Maen-bras   Thick Stone   OS Ref 581 551
After ascending the initial zigzags of the Snowdon Ranger path, the track levels off and Llechog Facet is clearly visible to the right. In the foreground is the fine boulder of Carreg Maen-bras with about a dozen boulder-problems ranging from 4b to 6b. All are on the solitary boulder and give excellent climbing. A perfect place for some extra sport on the way home from Llechog, or even for the main feast itself.

Craig Allt Maenderyn   Bird Rock Crag   OS Ref 599 523
A small crag in a majestic position with fine views of Yr Aran and Moel Hebog. Being south-facing it is perfectly placed to receive lots of sun, but also somewhat exposed to the prevailing wind. The rock is excellent, with strange horizontal striations giving pleasant climbing to those in search of solitude and esoterica.

Leave the Rhyd Ddu car-park (pay and display) by the Snowdon path but, instead of following the main path towards Llechog, continue east towards Bwlch Cwm Llan until a quarry hole on the left of the path is reached at OS Ref 602 522 with a small shed nearby. Go up the hillside past the shed; the crag is soon clearly visible in front and reached in a few minutes across the boggy hillside.

At the base of the crag is a detached flake, 6 metres to the right of which is a slim corner.

Jug Rehab   18 metres   E2   5b   (9.01)
Climb the slim corner with some difficulty, and then head straight up the bold slab to the top.

Nexus 6   18 metres   E2   5c   (9.01)
Three metres right of *Jug Rehab* is a vague corner and crackline, which is followed with interest, particularly at the steep start, to an *in-situ* thread. Above, follow the flakes on the slab to the top.

Chwarel Ffridd Isaf   Lower Enclosure Quarry OS Ref 572 526
A small quarry hole 10 minutes up the Snowdon path from the car-park in Rhyd Ddu. The quarry is easily seen on the right-hand side of the path. This seemingly insignificant and somewhat ugly hole in the ground has been the subject of controversy of late as the Welsh Highland Railway Company wanted to fill it with waste. It appears, however, that the quarry is a significant landmark in Welsh literature, as the writer T H Parry-Williams refered to it in his essay *Hen Chwareli* (*Old Quarries*).

Some easier lines, no longer definable, were climbed here in the late 60s. The first two of the more recent routes are found on the slab on the left and the third is located in the hanging corner at the back right of the quarry. While the climbing is not of the finest quality, there are a number of bolts, so the place may appeal to some slateheads bored of the Vivian or sport

Llechog

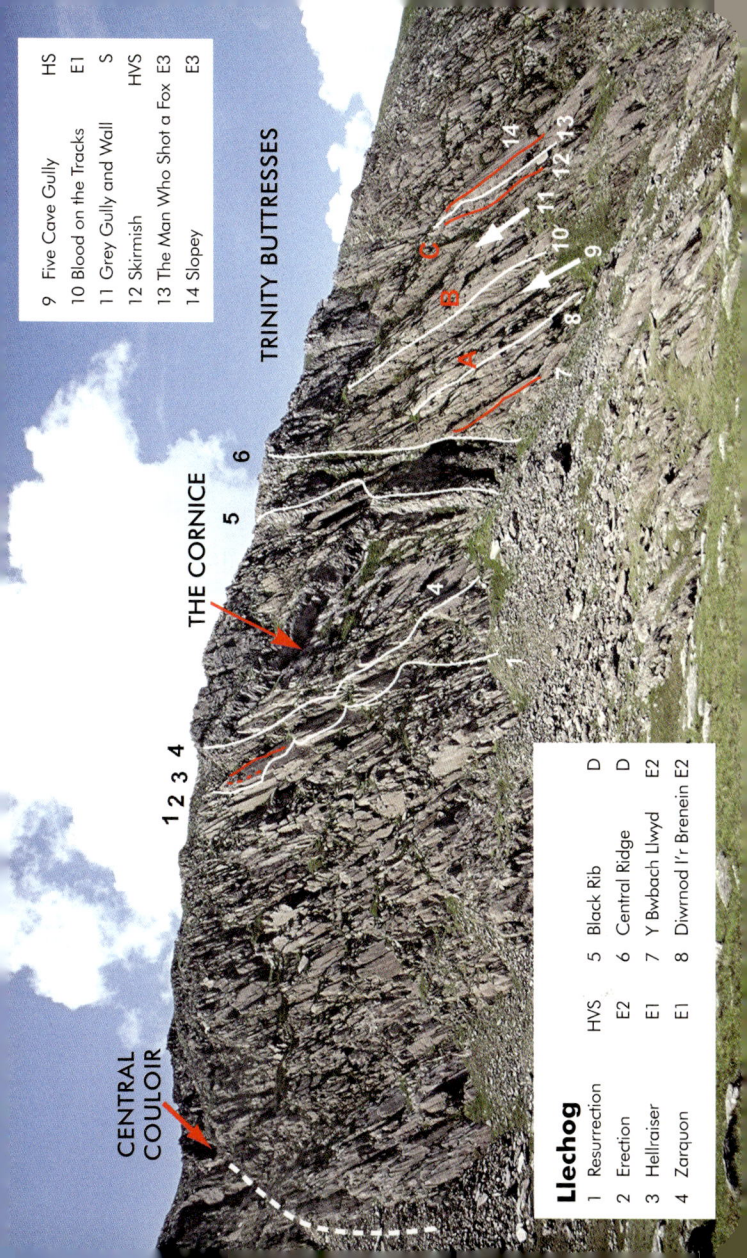

1	Resurrection	HVS
2	Erection	E2
3	Hellraiser	E1
4	Zarquon	E1
5	Black Rib	D
6	Central Ridge	D
7	Y Bwbach Llwyd	E2
8	Diwrnod I'r Brenein	E2
9	Five Cave Gully	HS
10	Blood on the Tracks	E1
11	Grey Gully and Wall	S
12	Skirmish	HVS
13	The Man Who Shot a Fox	E3
14	Slopey	E3

CENTRAL COULOIR

THE CORNICE

TRINITY BUTTRESSES

Extreme Unction (E3)
Craig Planwydd
(first ascent, 2003)
Climber:
Paul Jenkinson
Photo: Terry Taylor

Gael Forces (HVS), Clogwyn y Garreg (first ascent, 2003) (Craig y Bera on left) Climber: Terry Taylor Photo: Taylor col.

Llechog Facet

#	Route	Grade
1	Batelion	S
2	Bar Steward	VD
3	Chantilly Lace	E2
4	Another Green World	E3
5	Good Golly Miss Molly	E4
6	Shake, Rattle, and Roll	E4
7	Nadroedd	S
8	Residents' Wall	VS

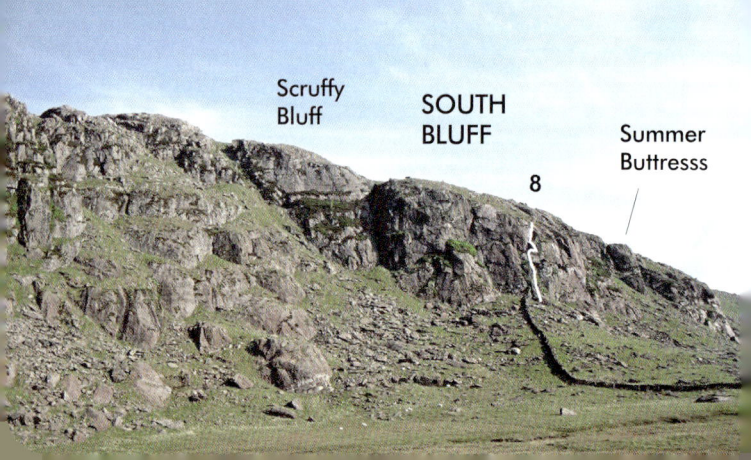

climbers who been have dragged screaming to Llechog. However, the biggest attraction must be the Wadworth's 6X in the nearby pub, especially considering the National Park car-park is pay-and-display!

Line of Best Fit   15 metres   E5 6b   (2.11.86)
Take a line up the centre of the slab past two bolts. Bold.

Pearly Dew Drops Drop   15 metres   E4 6a   (10.86)
At the right-hand side of the slab, climb past two bolts to the top (wires needed). Sadly, chipped.

Hanging Gardens of Demijohn   10 metres   F6a   (1993)
With four bolts in 5 metres this must be the safest and probably the easiest extreme in Wales, if not the universe. Start below the hanging corner and climb the loose bit to reach it. Follow the right wall, clipping every metre, to a belay over the top.

Dyffryn Nantlle & Cwm Silyn

Dyffryn Nantlle is the quiet valley that runs in an easterly direction from Penygroes. The lower half of the valley is dominated by the old slate workings, but once past Llyn Nantlle Uchaf the valley becomes more peaceful and is little frequented.

Most of the crags here are for the lover of solitude. Even the Cwm Silyn group, the most popular, is unlikely to attract more than a dozen parties on a fine summer weekend. This is not to decry the quality of the climbing: tastes change and none of the crags has sufficient routes to entertain a team climbing at a given standard for much more than a weekend. The area seems to suffer from an 'I ought to go there some time' attitude.

As will be noted in the introductions to some of the crags, the rock can leave much to be desired in certain places, areas of Craig y Bera in particular. With care and a little common sense, this augments rather than detracts from the experience found here. Like others in the area, these are mountain crags; they are susceptible to all the vagaries of the weather and it is not unknown for the occasional hold to join its brethren at the foot of the crag.

Please note that the access situation regarding most of the crags described in the valley is delicate and that only those approaches described should be used, even if they do appear to be circuitous.

Nantlle Slate Quarries

Spread along the hillside between the village of Talysarn and the small hamlet of Nantlle are a series of mainly abandoned slate workings. The last working area is slated for closure in the near future. There is only a little climbing at

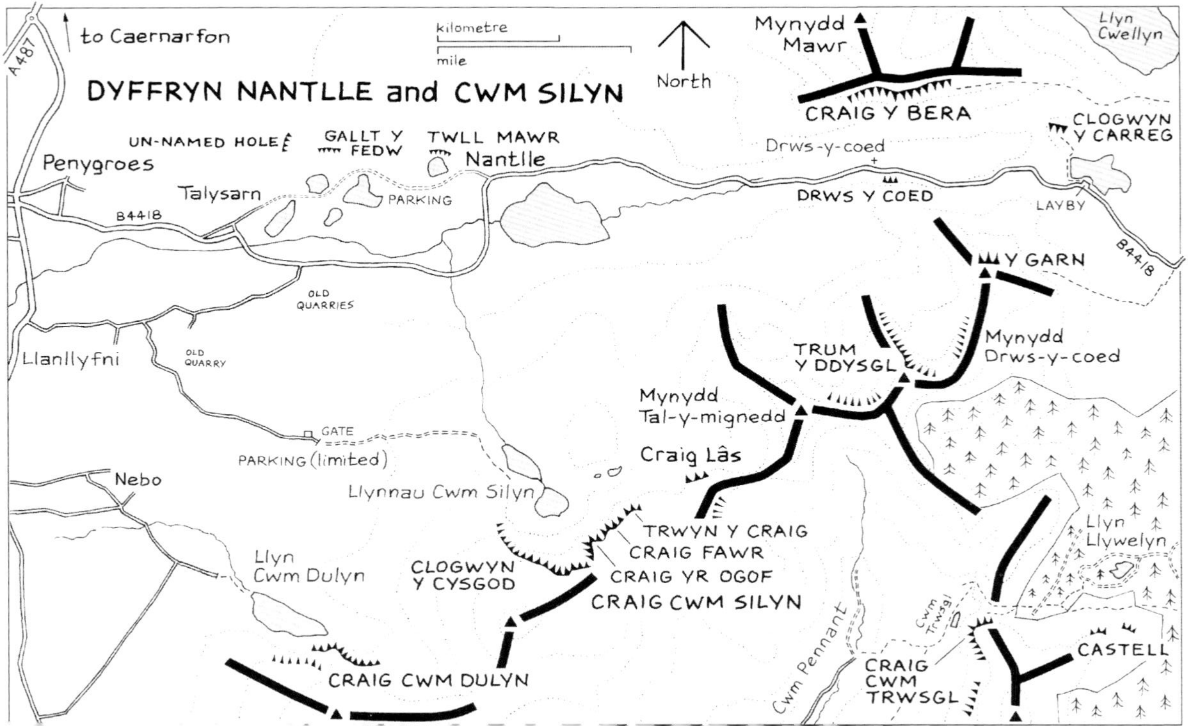

to Caernarfon
A487
kilometre
mile
North
DYFFRYN NANTLLE and CWM SILYN
Mynydd Mawr
CRAIG Y BERA
Llyn Cwellyn
CLOGWYN Y CARREG
UN-NAMED HOLE
GALLT Y FEDW
TWLL MAWR
Nantlle
Drws-y-coed
DRWS Y COED
LAYBY
Penygroes
Talysarn
PARKING
B4418
Y GARN
OLD QUARRIES
OLD QUARRY
Llanllyfni
TRUM Y DDYSGL
Mynydd Drws-y-coed
Mynydd Tal-y-mignedd
GATE
PARKING (limited)
Craig Lâs
Nebo
Llynnau Cwm Silyn
TRWYN Y CRAIG
CRAIG FAWR
CRAIG YR OGOF
CRAIG CWM SILYN
CLOGWYN Y CYSGOD
Llyn Cwm Dulyn
Llyn Llywelyn
Cwm Trwsgl
Cwm Pennant
CRAIG CWM TRWSGL
CASTELL
CRAIG CWM DULYN

present in these relics of a bygone era, and what currently exists is hardly great advertising for the slate-climbing art. Those routes worth seeking out are marked with a single star. Dynamite is too good for the others!

There are three areas developed, one of which, curiously, is not slate but dolerite. The expansion bolt makes its only appearance in the valley here.

All the workings that are of interest to the climber are most easily accessed from Nantlle, around five kilometres east of Penygroes, by taking the small lane leaving the main B4418 road at OS Ref 509 534.

This lane heads in a westerly direction, passing Twll Mawr (OS Ref 505 534) and Twll Balast (OS Ref 504 534 – not named on the map), until the large, flooded Dorothea Quarry is reached. This also is not named on the current 1:25000 map but is situated at OS Ref 498 533. Note that this area is very popular with divers: a diving training-centre has been proposed for the quarry and you may have trouble parking. Dorothea is over 90 metres deep in places!

Unnamed Hole   OS Ref 497 535

A deep elliptical-shaped quarry with a small, dark pool situated beneath a steep wall. A slate incline rises to the north-east of the parking-area. Go up the incline to the first level. Traverse leftwards along the top of the huge retaining wall through an old shed to a grassy area in front of the next hole. Continue in the same direction past the descent into that quarry's base through another building and climb the waste slope that lies at the end of the level to the next level. Follow the edge of this round to the left until the quarry comes into view to the right. The prow of *Purple Tailed Love Fish* is obvious at the far end of the right-hand wall. Access the base of the hole by descending the steep slope at the point of arrival.

Defcon Stacks   35 metres   E5 †
A shocking route! In the west wall a deep chimney leads (if you are lucky) to a bay – all very loose.
1 15m. 5c. Climb the chimney – very serious.
2 20m. 5b. Climb the wall on the right-hand side of the bay to escape to the top of the quarry.

★Purple Tailed Love Fish   30 metres   E3 5c
On the east wall is a prominent narrow square prow. On its left-hand side is a stunning crackline the 'Left Wall' of slate. Climb the crack to where it veers rightwards, and finish directly up the wall.

Chwarel Gallt y Fedw   Ash Bluff Quarry   OS Ref 499 535

Approach as for the preceding area by going up the incline to the first level and traversing leftwards along the top of the huge retaining wall through an old shed to a grassy area in front of the next hole. All the routes are on the east-facing wall of the quarry. Descend with care to the quarry floor.

The Great Arête   27 metres
This is the obvious grooved arête at the left-hand end of the quarry. It has been climbed but no details have been forthcoming.

To the right is an area of hanging slabs with several lines of bolts threading their way through the gorse bushes. No precise details are given as even the first ascensionists are unable to recall them!

Ian's Route   25 metres   F7a+   (1992)
The left of the two lines on the slab to the right-hand side of the quarry.

The Great and Secret Show   25 metres   F7b   (1992)
The central line of the slab and the bulging wall above via five bolts to a lower-off.

Twll Mawr   Big Hole   OS Ref 505 534
This is the flooded hole immediately behind Nantlle Terrace. At the top of the first rise in the track leading from Nantlle there is the bed of an old tramway behind and to the right. Park here. Walk eastwards along the old line past Twll Balast (this quarry was once a chemical dumping ground – which fact should deter most from venturing into its recesses) and the flooded Twll Mawr soon comes into sight.

The crag can be clearly seen on the far side. Walk round to the right of the quarry to the top of the cliff and descend by abseil. The rock is dolerite, has excellent friction, faces south, and is a sun trap.

★Blodeuwedd   30 metres   E2   5c   (2.8.92)
Start at the foot of the obvious V-groove (*Erwaint*) and move diagonally left to a good spike runner. Make a difficult move up to gain the arête proper, and climb it (good nut placements on right) to its top. Enter the groove above (peg) and climb this to finish.

★Erwaint   30 metres   E2   5c   (11.9.92)
The obvious V-groove between the two ribs. The climb can be quite dirty as a result of earth being washed down, so be prepared to clean out the cracks as you go. Climb the groove, passing a small overhang, to a steepening. Make an awkward move across the slab to the left to join *Blodeuwedd*. From the peg on that route, move left and climb the arête, finishing on good holds.

★Oars Moses   24 metres   E3   6b   (6.83)
The central rib offers a technical start, a bold middle, and a strenuous finish! Good climbing. Ascend the right-hand corner/groove (large camming devices) for 5 feet. A difficult move left gains the arête. Climb the thin crack and then the arête to a good spike at the foot of the final overhanging crack, which leads to the top.

The right-hand corner/groove is Very Severe but leads to an overgrown bay and is not recommended.

Craig y Bera   Kite Crag   OS Ref 545 540

Mynydd Mawr possesses three cliffs on its slopes, of which this is not everyone's favourite. A vast ruinous cliff, Craig y Bera is something of an acquired taste. Forming a complex mass of pinnacled ridges and steep gully walls, the cliff dominates the northern side of Dyffryn Nantlle between Nantlle and Rhyd Ddu. The rock varies in quality from atrocious to excellent and the worthwhile routes range from easy mountaineering ridges, through the classic *Angel Pavement*, to big adventures in the Extreme grades.

Craig y Bera does offer good views and interesting features to those able to cope with the capricious nature of the rock, which can be loose on both large and small scales. Multiple belays are advisable as even apparently solid rock may disintegrate under load.

The grades should be treated with caution since, apart from *Angel Pavement*, which is relatively solid and well used, most of the traditional routes see few ascents and much depends on the individual climber's capability in handling poor material. On a more positive note, the rock on the harder routes is generally good, and a south-facing aspect means that the crag dries quickly and gives good climbing conditions for much of the year.

The upper area of the crag was the scene of a plane crash in the late 60s and debris may be discovered over a wide area.

Direct access to this cliff from Drws y Coed, although commencing on a right-of-way, is appreciated by neither the farmer nor one's knees. The simplest means of access, and not as circuitous as it first appears, is to park one kilometre north of Rhyd Ddu, at the south-east end of Llyn Cwellyn by the forestry entrance. Take the footpath leading across the meadow from the first gate and continue in the same line through the woods to gain open land. Follow the path up Mynydd Mawr along the side of the trees to the highest point of the wood, from where it is possible to contour across the hillside to beneath the cliff. (30 to 40 minutes.) A drystone wall leads from the valley to abut the crag at the foot of the *Angel Pavement* buttress.

Descent of most of the intervening gullies is possible, though the cautious may wish to continue to the main ridge and take the long way down. The routes in the *Angel Pavement* area finish atop the prominent pinnacle well seen in profile on the approach. From here, it is possible to descend to the left (facing in) via an exposed path and gully leading to scree.

The wide central buttress of *Pinnacle Ridge*, with a stone wall rising to it, dominates the scene. On its right, across a scree-filled descent gully, is *Sentries' Ridge*. On the left of *Pinnacle Ridge* and at a higher level is a smaller, loose(!) buttress, which contains two routes. Diagram page 56b.

Reason in Revolt   102 metres   Hard Severe   (22.6.52)
If the name doesn't put you off, then start at the foot of a slabby area, below and to the left of the small buttress.

1 27m. Follow steep and loose rock, right of heather, to a large belay.
2 12m. Continue in the same line on better rock.
3 15m. Go across a grassy rake; then climb more steeply to a stance with two spike belays.
4 30m. Take a chimney-crack on the right to a heather field; then follow the steep and loose rib on its left with difficulty to a break and poor belays.
5 18m. Continue steeply to the top and safety.

No Highway   75 metres   Hard Severe   (17.3.52)
A fair route on better rock than its neighbour. Start at the foot of the right-hand edge of the buttress.
1 15m. Climb the left-hand side of the ridge to a ledge.
2 15m. Move back left onto the face and climb to another ledge beneath a line of overhangs.
3 21m. Go directly up to the overhang and round it on the left to gain a fine exposed leftwards traverse. Follow this to reach a ledge, which leads back to the right-hand edge.
4 24m. Go easily to the top.

To the right is the main buttress of Craig y Bera, known as Pinnacle Ridge, giving the best climbing on the cliff. The buttress contains a series of slabby rakes interspersed with steep walls building up rightwards to the crest of the ridge. Its most obvious feature is a huge triangular slab, which is taken by the start of *Angel Pavement*. The corners taken by *The Sceptic* and *Guardian Angel* lie on the hanging wall up and right of the triangular slab. Diagram page 56b.

The Devils   112 metres   E3   (15.5.98)
A good varied route taking a series of grooves in the steep rock below *Angel Pavement*, then a big corner above it. Start on a projecting rock spur below an obvious crack in the lower walls, some 70 metres above and to the left of the start of *Angel Pavement*.
1 15m. 5a. Gain and climb the crack; then bear left to belay at some pointed flakes.
2 18m. 5c. Climb the smooth groove above, then a crack leading left. Continue to a restricted stance in a corner below a roof.
3 12m. 5a. Step up, shun the loose corner ahead, and traverse right along a narrow slab until it is possible to climb direct to a stance on *Angel Pavement*.
4 37m. 5c. Enter the big corner above from the right, climb to the obvious jammed flake, and then step right to a narrower corner, which leads to easy-angled rock.
5 30m. Easy climbing up the left edge of the buttress.

☆☆**Voice in the Wilderness**   121 metres   E5 †   (16.4.97)
The major challenge of the cliff, giving bold and strenuous climbing on good rock until the very top. It takes the steep walls left of *Angel Pavement* and crosses it for pitch 3. Between the spur under *The Devils* and the gully leading to *Y Credwr* is a short smooth wall with a thin crack in its centre. Start here.

1 24m. 5c. Follow the thin crack to a ledge above the wall. Easier ground leads to good belays in a corner-crack below the smooth curving groove in the barrier above.
2 30m. 6a. Climb the groove and its left arête to the obvious flake. Continue through the apex of the groove until the difficulties ease. Trend left for 6 metres; then climb straight up through a small groove to a stance on *Angel Pavement*.
3 37m. 6b. Left of the big corner of *The Devils* is a slimmer groove. Enter it from the left to gain holds and a good runner on the right, and then an obvious foothold in the left wall. Sustained climbing up the groove and flake above leads to a final steep wall and a cautious exit via a small groove.
4 30m. Easy ground leads left to the top of the buttress.

☆☆**Y Credwr**   104 metres   E4 †   (31.3.97)
An enjoyable route on good rock throughout. Scramble up the gully on the left of *Angel Pavement* to belay at a corner beneath a steep buttress.
1 37m. 6a. Climb a thin crack up the nose of the buttress until it becomes a deeper crack heading right. Continue up this crack a short distance; then step back left above the bulge and go up a groove to the edge of the *Angel Pavement* slab. Climb up 3 metres; then trend easily right to belay in the big corner.
2 37m. 6a. Climb the large smooth corner above and the continuation grooves to reach a sloping ledge below the big roof. Exciting moves rightwards beneath the roof gain an exposed shelf, then easier ground. Belay 3 metres higher.
3 30m. Trend leftwards up the broken buttress.

★**Angel Pavement**   183 metres   Severe   (5.7.46)
An excellent route, but recommendable only to confident parties as protection is poor, the rock is often questionable, and the pitches are long. The route follows the narrow gangway slipping past the steep walls in the centre of the buttress in positions of high exposure. Start at the foot of the expanse of slab, some 30 metres left of the drystone wall abutting the crag.
1 46m. Climb the slab, towards the left where it is easiest, but everywhere with a striking lack of protection, to a large grassy terrace. Thread belay at its right-hand end.
2 46m. Climb diagonally left across the steep slab on good holds; then continue directly up the undulating slab to a second grassy ledge below an overhang. Thread belay in the crack on the right.
3 30m. Follow the narrow rib to the left of the overhang in a fine exposed position; then climb more broken rock to a small ledge.
4 46m. Climb the rib on the left and go up to grass. Continue into a corner and trend left beneath steep walls to reach ledges.
5 15m. Continue up more broken rock to the top.
A pointless variation at Very Severe, avoiding the best of the route, follows the steep slab leading rightwards from the top of pitch 2 to gain easy ledges and *Pinnacle Ridge*. A variation finish takes the groove with a jammed flake at half height to the left of the normal finish at Very Severe 4b.

★The Sceptic   138 metres   E2   (22.5.95)
This is the left-hand of the two grooves in the hanging wall overlooking *Angel Pavement*. Positions and protection are better than on *Guardian Angel*. Start as for *Angel Pavement*.
1 46m. 4c. Climb the slab, taking the most interesting line, to the large grassy terrace and thread belay on the right.
2 46m. 5b. Climb to a peg below the groove of *Guardian Angel*. Move up into the left-hand groove and climb it to a difficult but well-protected exit. Continue straight up the edge of the buttress to spike belays.
3 46m. Wander up the buttress above.

Guardian Angel   76 metres   E3   (19.9.70)
A serious route taking the more prominent, right-hand of the two grooves in the steep wall overlooking *Angel Pavement*. Start on the grassy ledge at the top of the first pitch of *Angel Pavement* and *The Sceptic*, and below small twin grooves leading to the right-hand and more obvious groove.
1 15m. Climb either of the small grooves to belay on a large detached block.
2 37m. 5c. Move directly into the main (right-hand) groove and climb it with difficulty past two pegs until a line of holds leads left to the arête. Follow this to a small ledge, move up left, and then make a rising traverse back right on disposable holds (loose blade runner) to the arête and the security of pitch 4 of *Primrose Path*. Follow this to a grassy ledge.
3 24m. *Primrose Path* pitch 5.

Primrose Path   134 metres   Very Difficult   (16.10.49)
This route takes the narrow slab above and parallel to *Angel Pavement*, giving a good open route after a poor start. Start right of *Angel Pavement* in the second bay to the left of the drystone wall abutting the crag.
1 43m. Climb a heathery corner until it divides; then follow the vegetated right-hand branch to a large grassy ledge. This point can be reached more pleasantly by climbing the first pitch of *Angel Pavement* and traversing right.
2 21m. Amble up the fields on the right to a cave below a groove.
3 20m. Start up the left wall of the groove; then climb a slab up leftwards until it is possible to move back to a grassy ledge at the top of the groove.
4 26m. Traverse out onto the left edge of the slab overlooking *Angel Pavement*, and follow this airily to a hidden grass ledge above.
5 24m. Follow the ledge up left until a short corner and wall above lead to a sudden finish on scree.
Some 50 metres of loose scrambling remains to the top of *Pinnacle Ridge*.
Perdition Finish
Another nice pitch and a nasty one. Really no more than Very Difficult though the objective dangers on the last pitch make it Very Severe overall.
6 30m. From the top of pitch 5, go to the left edge of the buttress and follow it to a rock ledge via pleasant exposed climbing.
7 21m. Above, everything is horrid. Go up and left a bit to the edge. Climb over rattling rocks and finish up vertical scree.

Voice in the Wilderness (E5)
Craig y Bera (first ascent, 1997)
Climber: Pat Littlejohn
Photo: Littlejohn col.

Craig y Bera

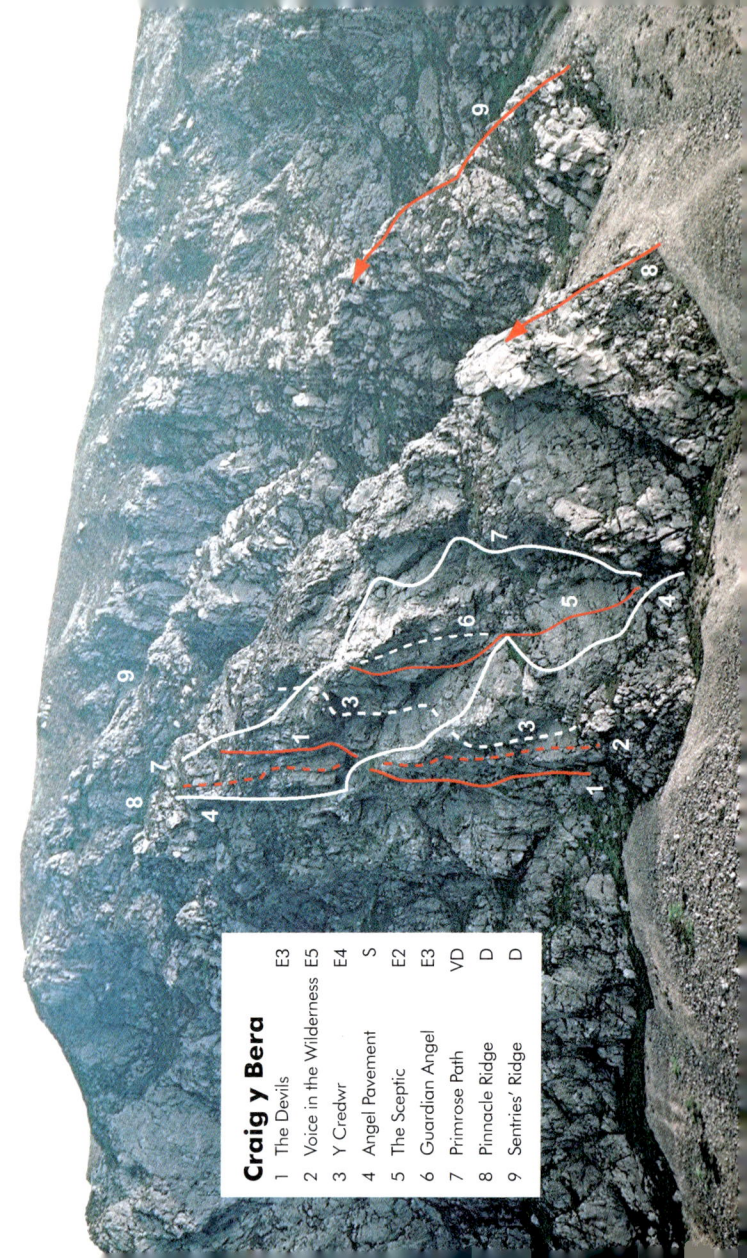

1. The Devils — E3
2. Voice in the Wilderness — E5
3. Y Credwr — E4
4. Angel Pavement — S
5. The Sceptic — E2
6. Guardian Angel — E3
7. Primrose Path — VD
8. Pinnacle Ridge — D
9. Sentries' Ridge — D

Clogwyn y Garreg

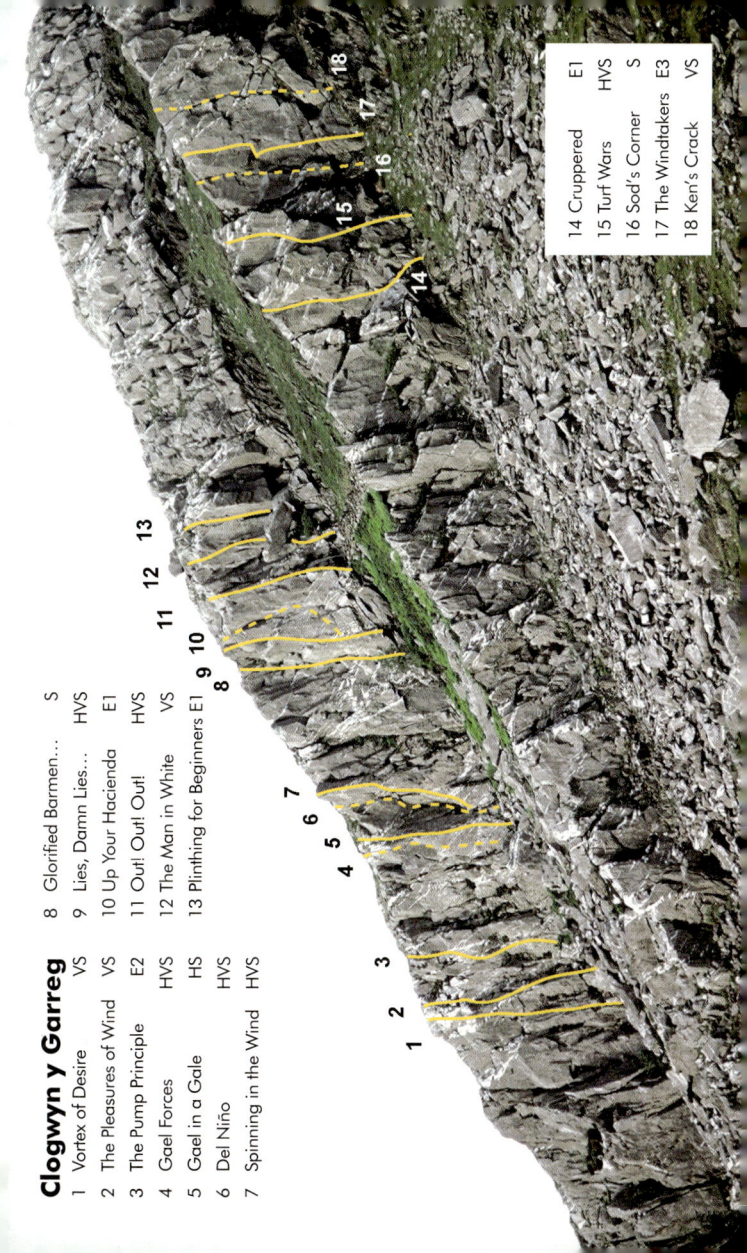

1 Vortex of Desire	VS
2 The Pleasures of Wind	VS
3 The Pump Principle	E2
4 Gael Forces	HVS
5 Gael in a Gale	HS
6 Del Niño	HVS
7 Spinning in the Wind	HVS
8 Glorified Barmen…	S
9 Lies, Damn Lies…	HVS
10 Up Your Hacienda	E1
11 Out! Out! Out!	HVS
12 The Man in White	VS
13 Plinthing for Beginners	E1
14 Cruppered	E1
15 Turf Wars	HVS
16 Sod's Corner	S
17 The Windtakers	E3
18 Ken's Crack	VS

Lech Drws y Coed

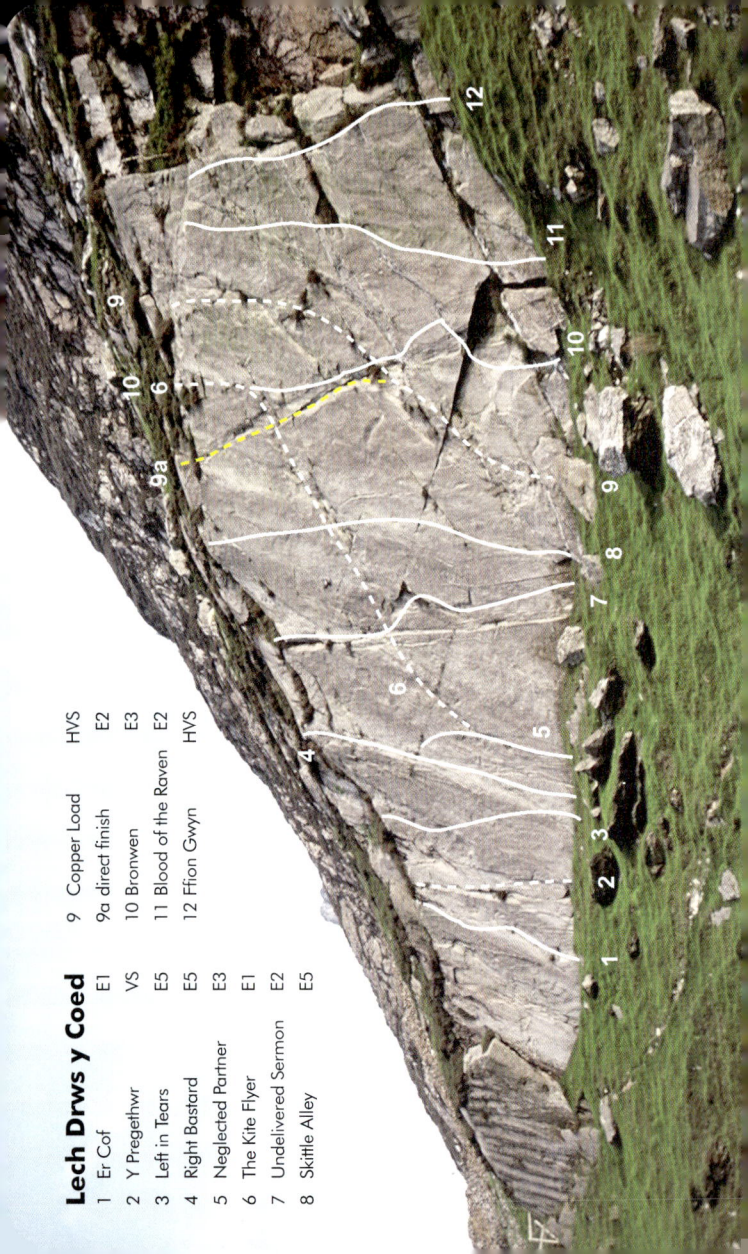

1 Er Cof	E1	9 Copper Load	HVS
2 Y Pregethwr	VS	9a direct finish	E2
3 Left in Tears	E5	10 Bronwen	E3
4 Right Bastard	E5	11 Blood of the Raven	E2
5 Neglected Partner	E3	12 Ffion Gwyn	HVS
6 The Kite Flyer	E1		
7 Undelivered Sermon	E2		
8 Skittle Alley	E5		

Pinnacle Ridge   120 metres   Difficult   (1905)
Pleasant and typical ridge-climbing, but rather loose in places. Start just left of the foot of the pinnacle that gives the route its name. Belays may be taken at suitable opportunities. Climb the pinnacle by either its left edge or the corner to the right. Continue up the ridge to the top.

The obvious spiky ridge on the far side of the descent gully gives:

Sentries' Ridge   110 metres   Difficult   (1910)
'The ridge is notched and carved into fourteen pinnacles or gendarmes. All yield to direct assault. The second involves a tricky horizontal traverse around an overhanging protuberance, with a stiff vertical chimney to follow. The ridge has a moderate average gradient, but some of the sites attained are singular, and, as each gendarme completely screens the rest, a certain unexpectedness is a feature of the climb.' (Archer Thomson's first-ascent description. For those who find this unexpectedness overwhelming, an easier way is usually possible to the right.)

Clogwyn y Garreg   Rock Crag   OS Ref 557 537

This is the set of slanting scarps seen at the head of Dyfryn Nantlle as one is heading over to Rhyd Ddu. It varies in height from 10 metres to around 25 metres. There are three parallel scarps, with climbs on the two lower ones.

Currently the landowner **does not permit climbing**. However, it is possible that this situation will change when CRoW is fully implemented and so the decision has been taken to include these descriptions. For the time being it is in all interests that the restriction is observed.

Park at a gate by the Llyn y Dywarchen ('turf lake') reservoir, taking care not to block it. Walk left around the lake and head up to the crag after crossing a stile.

Above the lake is a small broken crag with a slabby rib on its right-hand side:
The Magic Sod (17 metres Difficult † 21.9.97).

The second scarp has a stone wall dividing it in two, with a huge left-leaning plinth just to the right. Down to the left is a big streaked boulder below a neat slim slab, and further down and left is a prominent low arête, beyond which the crag quickly loses height. At the left-hand end, a coffin-shaped block leans against the edge.

Diagram page 56c.

Terry Tomb Tome   10 metres   Very Severe   4c †   (28.6.03)
Climb the block.

Another Day   15 metres   Hard Very Severe   5b †   (28.6.03)
Climb the cracked wall to the right of the block. Good micro-wire protection.

58 Dyffryn Nantlle

Vortex of Desire 15 metres Very Severe 4c † (9.5.03)
Start 4 metres right of the low arête, just down and left of an edge with a large block perched on its top. Good climbing leads directly up to the left edge of the block, which is then laybacked tremulously to the top.

The Pleasures of Wind 15 metres Very Severe 4b † (9.5.03)
The groove down and right of the perched block leads steadily up leftwards until level with the block. Finish directly up from this point.

The Pump Principle 15 metres E2 5c † (9.5.03)
Starts 2 metres right again at a bush below a recess. Go direct up to the recess, above which a good clean crack splits the face. Make tricky moves straight up for 3 metres before stepping right and finishing, more easily but boldly, directly up some quartz flakes.

Five metres further up the hill is the big streaked boulder.

Gael Forces 15 metres Hard Very Severe 5a † (9.5.03)
Step off the boulder onto the slab, which is taken direct on good small edges to a sloping ledge directly above. Finish easily once the ledge is gained.

Gael in a Gale 15 metres Hard Severe 4a † (9.5.03)
Begin up the open groove just right of the slab and trend leftwards to the right edge of the slab. Follow the edge direct to the top.

Del Niño 15 metres Hard Very Severe 5a † (9.5.03)
The open groove is followed past some big perched flakes to its top. Pull up onto the right wall and into the corner. An excellent crack leads peacefully to the top.

Spinning in the Wind 15 metres Hard Very Severe 5a † (9.5.03)
The arête to the right has a scruffy bottom so is best approached from the left. Start in the groove as for *Del Niño* but immediately step up and right onto the wall leading up to a flake crack. At the base of the crack, stretch right to the arête and swing boldly onto it. Follow the arête to the top.

Glorified Barmen with Attitude 15 metres Severe † (21.9.97)
Start at the base of a wide groove about 5 metres down and left of the stone wall. Go up on slopers (sparse gear) to cracks. Follow these to finish on jugs.

Lies, Damn Lies, and Statistics
15 metres Hard Very Severe 5b † (21.9.97)
Start at the base of the arête to the right of the preceding route. Climb this, mainly on its left-hand side.

Up Your Hacienda 15 metres E1 5c † (21.9.97)
Start as for *Lies, Damn Lies, and Statistics*. Move up and right along a handrail and pull through the bulge. Move up the cracked wall above to gain an obvious curving groove to finish.

Out! Out! Out!   15 metres   Hard Very Severe   5b †   (21.9.97)
Start just below the stone wall. Pull through the bulge on jugs to reach cracks. Climb these directly with fingery moves.

The Man in White   15 metres   Very Severe   4c †   (21.9.97)
Start just above the stone wall. Move up past flakes and to the right of a holly. Step back left to reach a crack leading up on the right-hand side of the arête.

Plinthing for Beginners   15 metres   E1   5b   (9.5.03)
The perfect steep crack in the corner behind the foot of the plinth. Begin 3 metres right of the stone wall and scramble up behind the leaning plinth. The crack is safe and leans more steeply near the top.

The lower scarp consists of two buttresses separated by a rocky, mossy gully.

☆**Cruppered**   15 metres   E1   5b †   (9.02)
Climb the obvious corner-crack 3 metres left of *Turf Wars*, using a variety of jams and laybacks.

To Rest Is to Rust   13 metres   E2   5b †   (28.6.03)
The overhanging block left of *Turf Wars*. Start by swinging in from the right at the base.

Turf Wars   14 metres   Hard Very Severe   5a †   (21.9.97)
The first crack from the right of the left-hand buttress. When the crack ends climb flakes to the top.

Sod's Corner   15 metres   Severe   4a †   (21.9.97)
The corner just right of the central gully.

☆☆**The Windtakers**   15 metres   E3   5c †   (21.9.97)
The prime route of the crag takes the centre of the wall on the left-hand part of the right-hand buttress. Excellent climbing with bombproof gear. Start a little to the right of a line of old nails. Pull awkwardly onto the sloping shelf and follow a thin crack until it is possible to step right at the overlap to reach the quartz crack. Continue direct to the top.

Ken's Crack   15 metres   Very Severe   4c †   (21.9.97)
Jam and layback the obvious crack in the right-hand buttress.

Play It Smooth   14 metres   Hard Very Severe   5b †   (28.6.03)
To the right of *Ken's Crack* is a hanging corner and a groove. Climb straight up, utilizing both. Beware the loose block.

At a slightly higher level on the opposite side of the hill-top, a delightful slab faces towards Moel Eilio, giving fine views of Craig y Bera. It accommodates the longest route on the crag: **In Search of Perpetual Motion** (20 metres Difficult 8.6.03).

Y Garn   The Cairn   OS Ref 551 526

This crag is seen in splendid outline from the road between Beddgelert and Rhyd Ddu. It consists of two ridges high on the slopes of Y Garn, both of which give excellent climbing in fine situations and provide appropriate ways of starting the traverse of the Nantlle Ridge.

The cliff is best approached from the public footpath leading from Rhyd Ddu to Cwm Pennant. Park in the National Park car-park in Rhyd Ddu and take the footpath on the opposite side of the road which leads generally west across a series of stepping stones to join the road leading to Nantlle. A little way along the road, where it bends rightwards, take the footpath south-west to Cwm Pennant until open ground is reached and the permitted path giving access to the Nantlle ridge branches to the right.

Follow the permitted path until well above the enclosed fields before turning rightward to gain a sheep-track that runs across the steep heathery ground between the broken crags and the scree below. Follow the sheep-track past the old stone wall that runs up to meet the crag; then turn up into the bay beneath the cliff. (About 45 minutes.)

Alternatively, and slightly longer in time, continue to the summit of Y Garn and descend Central Gully, which lies between *Eastern Arête* and *Mallory's Ridge*. The top of Central Gully is between the summit cairn and the stone wall.

The cliff can also be reached less directly from Dyffryn Nantlle by starting as for Craig Trum y Ddysgl on the right-of-way past Tal y Mignedd (page 63), and then contouring across the slopes of Y Garn.

A direct approach to the cliff from Bwlch Gylfin is not permitted by the farmer.

There is a **restriction** on the whole of this crag from one hour before sunset until sunrise, from August until November (inclusive). This is to prevent disturbance to roosting birds.

The cliff faces north and is liable to remain damp for long periods. The first route starts about 60 metres left of *Eastern Arête*, at the wall which runs up the hillside to meet the cliff.

Reunion Cracks   50 metres   Severe   [R]   (16.6.48)
This takes the steep and slimy black crack immediately above the wall. Not the best route in the world! Start from the wall and follow the crack, steeply at first, to a ledge at 15 metres. Climb the right-hand crack over the overhang to another possible stance. Steep but easy climbing remains.

★★**Eastern Arête**   123 metres   Very Difficult   [R]   (1905)
This fine and popular route on good rock takes the left ridge and offers a natural 'mountaineering' prelude to the Nantlle Ridge. There has been a recent rockfall below the final V-groove. Start at the edge of the ridge, just before the entrance to Central Gully on the right.

1 30m. Gain the body of the ridge, and climb a chimney and grooves to a stance beneath a nose.
2 9m. Climb the short steep nose to finish awkwardly on a sloping ledge.
3 24m. Climb the corner above to a slabby wall, and then go rightwards to a large ledge.
4 30m. Climb the awkward crack on the right and another steep wall above.
5 30m. Go easily up the edge for 24 metres and then climb a difficult final V-groove.
Scrambling remains.

★★**Mallory's Ridge**   114 metres   Hard Very Severe [R]   (9.11)
A good route giving excellent climbing at a reasonable standard, except for the fourth pitch, which, in less than perfect conditions, may require aid and even rejects many. The route follows the backbone of the ridge, which is to the right of the right-hand ridge as a whole. Start about 6 metres up to the right of the foot of the ridge.
1 15m. Climb a rib to the right-hand end of a wide heather ledge.
2 24m. Follow ledges up and rightwards, via some obvious spikes, into a groove on the edge of a steep slab, and continue to a small overhang. Swing back left to a good ledge on the front of the arête.
3 24m. Climb up for a couple of metres; then move out right to the edge above the steep slab and follow this and the groove above to another good ledge below a steep nose.
4 24m. 5a. Move round the edge to the right and make a rising traverse rightwards with increasing difficulty until it is possible to climb up past a small ledge to a terrace.
5 15m. Climb the crack in the wall above to a stance amongst the pinnacles that litter its top.
6 12m. Continue up the ridge to the summit cairn.
Variations
The crux can be avoided by a number of alternatives: the steep nose above the stance can be climbed direct – slightly easier but looser than the usual route; or a traverse left can be made to a large grassy ledge (belay possible), from which a short difficult corner is climbed to regain the original route at the terrace.

★**The End of History**   92 metres   E2 [R]   (6.95)
Start further up the gully from the base of *Mallory's Ridge* at an obvious wide crack. Graded for the damp conditions usually encountered.
1 37m. 5c. Enter and follow the crack (awkward) until it is necessary to pass some Damoclean blocks. Continue up to a stance on *Mallory's Ridge*.
2 46m. 5a. Continue directly up the arête to join the rest of *Mallory's Ridge*.
3 9m. Finish through the splinters.

Western Gully to the right of *Mallory's Ridge* contains no rock, and the Western Arête beyond is short and offers only broken scrambling.

Llech Drws y Coed   The Wood Pass Slab   OS Ref 543 534

This is the obvious slab above the Rhyd Ddu to Nantlle road. The routes are short but pack a lot in while they last. Diagram page 56d.

The land belongs to the Snowdonia National Park Authority: 'climbing is permitted at the individual's own risk, and it should be noted that rocks at the site may be unstable.' Seek **permission** from the farmer at Drws y Coed farm just to the north, and park 100 metres down the road opposite the new chapel. Cross the fence by the stile by the old ruin. At the time of writing access is not a problem provided permission is sought, but the farmer does not wish to see large and/or noisy groups here: centres, please note.

The rock is quite unusual, approaching fine granite in texture, and providing a style of climbing similar to that found on some continental granite crags.

The plaque beneath the crag commemorates the chapel that stood there until the prominent boulder descended from above. They obviously didn't pray hard enough!

Er Cof   11 metres   E1 5a   (1974)
Ascend the delicate scoops to the left of the crack at the left end of the crag to a difficult finishing-move.

Y Pregethwr   11 metres   Very Severe 5a   (1974)
The left-hand, peg-scarred crack leads pleasantly to an awkward finish.

Left in Tears   14 metres   E5 6b   (2.11.86)
Start just left of *Right Bastard*. Make difficult lunges to diagonal flakes. Step up to an obvious undercut flake. Place a skyhook for show and move up left with difficulty, then more easily to the top.

Right Bastard   14 metres   E5 6b   (2.11.86)
This is a direct start to *Neglected Partner*. Start just left of that route and follow the waterworn streak straight to the quartz break by some very trying moves. Skyhook and *RP0* at the crux. An intense experience.

★**Neglected Partner**   14 metres   E3 6a   (31.10.86)
Start 5 metres left of the central crack at a vague scoop. Climb this for 5 metres, with runners in the crack on the right. Step left across a quartz break leading to the pale streak, and go straight up it to the top.

The Kite Flyer   34 metres   E1 5c   (1974)
The obvious diagonal line starting left of centre. Start up *Neglected Partner* via a hard move and follow the curving ramp across *Undelivered Sermon* to finish away to the right.

★**Undelivered Sermon**   15 metres   E2 5c   (1974)
Start at the boulder in the centre of the crag with some difficult moves. Follow the crackline up to a small roof, and then go back left to finish up the continuation crack.

Skittle Alley 15 metres E5 6b (1986)
To the right of *Undelivered Sermon* is a smooth wall with a peg at two-thirds height. Start beneath the peg and wander up with hard moves to reach the break of *The Kite Flyer*. Step up past the peg and move leftwards to finish.

★Copper Load 21 metres Hard Very Severe 5b (1974)
This is the obvious crackline at the right-hand end of the crag, finishing to the right. The direct finish is E2. Note the interesting fixed gear.

Bronwen 23 metres E3 5c (21.7.97)
Start just left of the quartz-topped flake embedded in the ground. Move up to the overhang and pull through rightwards. Step left to join the base of the obvious crackline (*Copper Load*), move up right to a thin parallel slot, and finish direct. Low in the grade.

Blood of the Raven 23 metres E2 5c (1974)
Start just right of the quartz-topped flake. Move up to a quartzy ledge. Mantel the diagonal quartz seam above to reach good holds, which lead up rightwards to the base of a final clean slab. Ascend the right-hand side of the slab and move back left at the top. High in the grade.

Ffion Gwyn 21 metres Hard Very Severe 4c (21.7.97)
The right arête of the slab. Follow the arête on its front face with only just enough gear.

Craig Trum y Ddysgl   The Bowl Ridge Crag OS Ref 543 520

Craig Trum y Ddysgl is the large broken cliff tucked away in the secluded upper reaches of Cwm Tal y Mignedd below the summit of Trum y Ddysgl on the Nantlle Ridge. It is not really worth the walk unless one is in an exploratory frame of mind or seeking solitude. The cliff is generally vegetated, but less so on the right where two bands of lighter-coloured quartzite, separated by a shallow gully, provide the only routes.

The crag is subject to the same **bird restriction** as Y Garn (page 60).

The cliff can be approached from Dyffryn Nantlle by taking the right-of-way that leaves the road at OS Ref 524 534. Follow this through the lower pastures, passing Tal y Mignedd Uchaf and, after gaining the open hillside, trend left into the upper part of Cwm Tal y Mignedd.

South Buttress 140 metres Very Difficult [R] (5.20)
The left rib is wider and more quartz-marked than the other. It is broken by several grassy ledges and contains a prominent large slab high up. Start at the foot of the rib at the right-hand end of a ledge directly above a small cave. Climb a dirty groove on the right of the slabs to a cave at 18 metres and continue up the rib to a grassy ledge. A crack on the left leads to the foot of the large slab. Move left and climb a crack to gain the col behind a prominent tower on the left of the slab. Continue up the broken arête behind the tower to the top.

The Walkers' Pair 120 metres Very Severe [R] (5.9.96)
A mountaineering route in an obscure setting high above Dyffryn Nantlle. It takes a direct line up the right-hand rib. Start beneath the vertical quartz streaks.
1 18m. Climb directly up the vertical quartz streaks to pull into a niche. Follow steep rock, then grass to a belay in the middle of the pillar.
2 24m. Step right and climb a crack and groove capped by a massive flake of rock to a good belay just above.
3 24m. Climb steep grass and rock, aiming for the obvious big slab, to a belay below it.
4 24m. The slab. Step up and onto the slab and climb it directly before moving right onto the arête near the top. Continue to a huge chockstone belay.
5 30m. A short rocky wall behind the belay leads to easier ground.

North Buttress 120 metres Difficult [R] (5.20)
A fair climb. It avoids the main difficulties, though some of them may have been climbed by the early explorers. Start at the foot of the right-hand rib, between two patches of red rock.
1 12m. Climb straight up; then go leftwards to a grassy patch. The quartzy bulge above leads to a belay on the right.
2 21m. From the left-hand end of the ledge, climb a cracked nose to a platform overlooking the gully.
3 18m. Ledges lead into and up a large corner on the left of a thin rib. Gain the rib from a high ledge and climb it to a stance below a steep wall.
4 24m. Climb the wall to a ledge at 6 metres and scramble up to a belay at the foot of a steep slab level with the large slab on *South Buttress*.
5 12m. Move across to belay below the cleft on the left of the slab.
6 18m. Climb the cleft to the top of the slab.
7 15m. Easy climbing leads to the top of the buttress.
Scrambling leads to the top of the crag.

Cwmffynnon Spring[1] Valley OS Ref 537 515
The next cwm west from Cwm Tal y Mignedd. Seek permission at Tal y Mignedd Isaf farm and go past the upper buildings (Tal y Mignedd Uchaf) before passing onto the open hillside. Continue, ascending to the right to enter the cwm. The only recorded route here takes the gully splitting the crag behind the small llyn in the back of the cwm.

Main Left-Hand Gully 200 metres *Winter* III
Start at the lowest point of the buttress and follow the gully to a cave at around 80 metres. Exit via the left side of the cave, and continue in the same line to the summit of Mynydd Tal y Mignedd.

---

1 In the sense of a water source, not the season.

TRWYN Y GRAIG CRAIG FAWR CRAIG YR OGOF The Great Stone Shoot

CWM CISHEYN

to Craig tôs

Trwyn y Graig

1 Deep Chimney   D
2 Gardener's Gully   VD
3 The Recess Route   S
4 Overhanging Chimneys S
5 Terror Infirmer   S

Cwm Silyn   Spawning Lake Valley

Cwm Silyn lies on the northern side of the Nantlle Ridge, which separates Cwm Pennant and Dyffryn Nantlle, below the highest point on the ridge, Craig Cwm Silyn at 734 metres. The cwm is backed by an impressive arc of cliffs, nearly a mile in length, overlooking the moorland which slopes gradually down into Dyffryn Nantlle. The western end of the moorland drops slightly to form a post-glacial hollow, which is traditionally described as containing two lakes (though it is often possible to count three), and is dominated by the most impressive of the cliffs.

By car there are two means of approach to the road-head. First, from the main Caernarfon to Porthmadog road, the A487, turn off at Penygroes and head to Llanllyfni. In Llanllyfni take the road signposted to Tan yr Allt. The road to Bryn Gwyn is on the right about two-thirds of a mile from Llanllyfni at OS Ref 481 521. Second, when travelling down Dyffryn Nantlle along the B4418, turn left for Llanllyfni (signposted to Tan yr Allt) just before a small council estate. The road to Bryn Gwyn is on the left after about half a mile. Bryn Gwyn is about a mile and a half up this side road, which is narrow and leads to a gate at the end of the metalled surface. Cars should be left in the field just through the gate; take care not to block the track. This is private land so please do not drive across the field to save a few hundred metres of (easy) walking. The grassy track leads through three locked gates to some old mine ruins by Llynnau Cwm Silyn. From here, the path heads straight for Craig yr Ogof, with a final slog up the screes to the crag. (35 to 45 minutes.)

Note that in recent years some damage has occurred to vehicles parked in this vicinity: do not leave valuables in the car.

Another possible approach for those eager for a full mountain day is from Drws y Coed beneath Craig y Bera. Follow the second approach for Y Garn (page 60) onto the open mountainside. Above the upper farm buildings, turn right, and follow an old track round below Cwm Ffynnon into the valley of the Afon Craig-lâs. Near the head of this, bear up the slopes to the right and over the shoulder by two small marshy lakes into Cwm Silyn. This approach takes about 1½ hours, twice as long as the normal approach; however, it allows one to return by traversing the main ridge after a route.

There are four main cliffs in addition to this first, small, recently-visited crag.

Craig Lâs   Grey Rock   OS Ref 524 509

This lies in the unnamed cwm (of the Afon Craig-lâs) to the north-east of Cwm Silyn. The crag is also unnamed on the OS map and is not to be confused with the Craig Lâs on the south side of the Nantlle Ridge overlooking Cwm Pennant. Follow the main Cwm Silyn approach until it is possible to drop down and cross between the two lakes, and take a path slanting diagonally rightwards up the hillside. Cross the moor, passing two small, marshy lakes and, where the main path starts to climb up towards Bwlch Dros Bern (cairn), descend into the next cwm. The crag lies just beyond a stone wall and faces north.

Details of this crag were only received late in the production of the guide and have not been checked.

The main central buttress has a line of overhangs on its left side. On a grassy ledge about 15 metres up the crag is the large pointed pinnacle of *Vladophobia*.

The Mellow Misogynist 50 metres E2 † (23.8.02)
The good top pitch takes the fine crack in the hidden right wall of the central gully. Continuously interesting climbing which, apart from the upper traverse, is well protected. Start left of the grassy gully rising below the prominent central overhangs, and near a small rowan.
1 15m. 5a. Climb the central groove to an overhang. Pull out rightwards onto a slab and cross vegetation to belay at the foot of the upper wall.
2 35m. 5b. Climb the corner for 5 metres, step right, and make a long reach for a pocket. Continue up the sustained crack to a ledge. Move up and then traverse delicately leftwards across a slab to a large pocket. Climb the rib above to a final pull across the steep wall. Belay well back (50-metre rope required to reach a good spike).

Vladophobia 45 metres Hard Very Severe † (26.9.99)
A good top pitch with quite bold and worrying climbing above the large pinnacle. Start right of the leftward-slanting grassy gully, immediately below the main crest of the buttress.
1 15m. 4b. Climb the lower wall on its left side and move up rightwards to belay just to the right of the pinnacle.
2 30m. 5a. Climb onto the pinnacle and step onto the wall. Move up to a groove and a good spike runner. Continue up the groove with limited protection.

Kelled Crack 45 metres E1 † (26.9.99)
1 15m. 4b. *Vladophobia* pitch 1.
2 30m. 5b. Climb the crack behind the belay, and then the continuation rib.

Trwyn y Graig The Nose Crag OS Ref 520 505

Lying around 300 metres east of Craig Fawr, this small and rather broken crag rises out of the heather above two small marshy lakes on the shoulder to the east of Llynnau Cwm Silyn. It forms the left-most area of rock visible from the path above the main lakes. The crag is connected to the hillside by a slim grassy arête, which provides a fine finish to the routes. The summit plateau, marked by a tower-like cairn, is about 75 metres above the top of the crag.

Diagram page 64b.

Follow the main approach to Cwm Silyn until it is possible to drop down to the two lakes and pass between them. Take a path slanting diagonally rightwards across the hillside and, at the twin marshy lakes (mentioned in the alternative approach), scramble up heather slopes to the foot of the crag.

A broad heather terrace, The Heather Belt, runs across the crag about 15 metres up. In the centre there is a shallow gully, The Recess, while to the right is a fine nose of rock that gives the crag its name. This latter lies above the remains of a WW II plane which failed to negotiate the hillside.

Those eager for the full mountain experience will find a fine bivouac shelter in the boulders between this crag and Craig Fawr.

Descent is easily effected to either side of the crag.

Deep Chimney 41 metres   Difficult (12.4.25)
A deep-cut chimney between vertical walls is conspicuous just above The Heather Belt on the extreme left of the crag. A poor route, being a succession of avoidable pitches. Start below the chimney in an alcove guarded by a detached column.
1 12m. The Heather Belt is reached by a crack and an easy rib.
2 15m. Climb to the foot of the chimney.
3 14m. The chimney lands you on the broad ridge that runs along the top of the crag.
A further 45 metres of pleasant scrambling takes you to the summit ridge.

Gardener's Gully 48 metres   Very Difficult (5.6.49)
This route climbs The Recess, which *The Recess Route* leaves near the bottom. The climb can be a bit damp. Start from The Heather Belt, at the bottom of The Recess.
1 21m. Go straight up the gully, easy at first, then with two difficult chimneys to a belay.
2 9m. Traverse right to a rush-covered platform at the foot of a 4-metre crack.
3 18m. Climb the crack, which leads to the top of The Closet, 'a damp enclosure with four walls but no roof', and bear left up two short cracks to the summit.
Variation
2a Traverse left to a belay at an isolated block below a 10-metre gully.
3a Climb either by the rib on the left of this gully or by the rocks on the right and out at the top.

The Recess Route 63 metres   Severe (1925)
After gaining The Heather Belt below The Recess, this route goes out right to finish up the slanting groove on the left of the final nose of the buttress. The lower part of the route is poor, but the upper section is pleasant, though not nearly as good as *Overhanging Chimneys*. Start below The Heather Belt and immediately below The Recess.
1 15m. Go up a little rib to The Heather Belt.

2 21m. Climb easily up The Recess for 6 metres and then follow the right wall to a ledge. The short chimney on the right leads to another ledge.
3 9m. Climb a difficult crack in the wall above to a small ledge and then squeeze right into The Closet.
4 18m. Escape up a short crack on the right; then trend rightwards up the slanting break to the ledge at the top.

The next climb is the best on the cliff and maintains a high level of interest to the top.

★Overhanging Chimneys   100 metres   Severe   (10.4.25)
An old-fashioned and somewhat artificial route, but well worthwhile and on excellent rock. Start at the lowest point of the cliff, to the right of the final nose.
1 21m. Climb up leftwards to a huge leaning flake; then go diagonally right up the wall above to The Heather Belt.
2 24m. Maurice's Crack. Climb up leftwards to reach the foot of the right-hand crack in the wall above and follow this with interest until a traverse leads left to a stance below the first overhanging chimney.
3 12m. Struggle awkwardly up the chimney to a ledge.
4 20m. Climb the steep crack just right of the corner and then the rib above to a ledge. Ascend the second overhanging chimney to a ledge.
5 23m. Step round to the right into a groove and go up this until it steepens. Move right and climb the third overhanging chimney until a steep crack on the left leads to the top of the nose.
Scrambling remains.
There are many variations to the original route, which indeed goes out of its way to find difficulties, but none is worthy of description except for the direct finish:

Terror Infirmer   Severe
5a 21m. A good exposed pitch up the front of the nose from the stance at the top of pitch 4. Climb the flake in the chimney above the belay and move up left to the foot of a groove. Follow this to easy ground and the top.

Tower Chimney   63 metres   Difficult
A broken route situated at the right-hand end of the cliff. Start beneath the obvious pillar half-way up the cliff.
1 24m. Climb easy rocks near the right-hand end of the cliff to The Heather Belt.
2 9m. Climb the tall pillar by the strenuous cleft behind it.
3 30m. Easy climbing leads to a chimney and crack near the top of *Overhanging Chimneys*.

The Scarf   Very Difficult   (28.8.28)
A girdle of the crag above The Heather Belt. Although the rock is generally good and some steep ground is crossed, there is little worthwhile independent climbing. Climb pitch 2 of *Tower Chimney*, step onto the vertical wall, and climb a short, shallow chimney to a belay. Traverse left

near the top of the wall and continue beneath a rock canopy to a corner. Walk to a belay at the top of pitch 2 of *Overhanging Chimneys*, and climb the first overhanging chimney above. From the stance, a short scramble up and left leads to *The Recess Route*. Descend the right wall of The Recess and cross it to the other wall about 8 metres up. Climb a shallow chimney for 6 metres to a stance. A big step up and a careful move left lead to splendid belays a metre or two higher. Go round a sharp rib on the left to the end of difficulties.

Craig Fawr Big Crag   OS Ref 518 502

Although the largest of the Cwm Silyn crags, Craig Fawr is rather broken and easy-angled. It offers long easy mountaineering routes with many grassy and heathery ledges, but that are nevertheless on good rock.

The cliff is separated from Craig yr Ogof to the right by a wide couloir. The main part of the cliff consists of a long narrow buttress which slants up from right to left and is bounded on both sides by grassy gullies. The deeper, right-hand gully (*Prow Gully*) is separated from the wide couloir by a subsidiary buttress. See page 72a for diagram.

The cliff is reached from the 'twin' lakes via the scree slope which descends from its left-hand bounding gully. About 15 metres up this gully a faint path contours the heather ledges at the base of the cliff, linking it to Trwyn y Graig to the left and Craig yr Ogof to the right.

Descent is possible by either of the grassy gullies mentioned above or via the main couloir.

Non-Engineers' Climb   107 metres   Difficult   (5.31)
Start 30 metres above and to the left of *Engineers's Climb*.
The rib is climbed for 45 metres to where it terminates in a prominent square-cut tower. Crawl round the edge below the tower to a nest of bollards (not above suspicion) and a large belay. Climb the tower via the crack on the left, and take the easy section above, first right and then left. A final 15 metres of attractive climbing finishes with a wall.

Engineers' Climb   182 metres   Very Difficult   (10.4.25)
A good long route following the obvious line up the crest of the main buttress. The easiest line can be hard to follow but all the major difficulties can be turned. Start about 50 metres above the scree where the left-hand gully becomes more defined and starts to slant to the left.
1 21m. Climb a short groove and the crack above; then follow the rib on the right to a large ledge.
2 24m. From 6 metres right of the gully, move up left and onto a small ledge. Step left and go up a wide crack; then traverse right and climb a short groove which leads to easier ground. Ascend this to a ledge.
3 40m. Make a rising traverse left until overlooking the gully; then climb direct to a pinnacle. From the grassy ledge above, follow more ledges up left until it is possible to regain the crest of the buttress to the right. Go

round the edge and up sloping ledges to belay below a short wall and two obvious towers.
4 18m. Climb the crack in the corner of the left tower to easy ground, and go up left to belay below a short step.
5 30m. Ascend the step and the one above; then easy scrambling leads to a large terrace below the final tier.
6 34m. Climb to the foot of the square-cut tower above. Traverse a short distance right to a cleft and follow this and slanting cracks in the wall above to the top of the tower.
7 15m. Scrambling leads to a cairn.
Forty-five metres of scrambling leads to the top.

The next climb is short and begins high on the right wall of the final tier. It is best approached from the top of the cliff, down the gully between the main buttress and the subsidiary buttress to its right.

Bankers' Buttress 46 metres   Severe   (5.39)
Pleasant if a bit obscure. Start about 45 metres down from the top of the gully and a few yards right of an obvious grassy terrace.
1 34m. Move out left; then climb straight up to a small ledge. Follow a fault sloping up right to a narrow grassy ledge. Move right and climb up to a narrow slab leading to a corner.
2 12m. Climb up the slab, difficult at first, to the top.

Prow Gully   250 metres   *Winter* II
The gully on the right-hand side of the crag. Indistinct lower down.

The subsidiary buttress on the right of the main cliff is taken by the pleasant but indefinite **L.M.H.** (120 metres Moderate 1925).

Broad Gully   250 metres   *Winter* I
The gully just left of the main couloir separating Craig Fawr from Craig yr Ogof. It is better defined higher up before it broadens into a snow bowl.

Craig yr Ogof   The Cave Crag   OS Ref 517 501
This is by far the best and most popular of the Cwm Silyn crags, offering a wide variety of climbing in fine mountain situations. The crag is described in a number of sections, which differ in their climbing characteristics in terms of geology, aspect, and the amount of drainage they receive.

From the lakes, the most prominent feature of the crag is the great nose of rock above the obvious central cave that gives the crag its name. The rush-covered Ogof Terrace runs left from the cave, dividing the face on that side of the Nose into two tiers. Two dark gullies (*Black* and *Green*) slant leftwards up the left-hand side of the lower tier to meet the Ogof Terrace where it finishes near the top of the right-hand gully.

The Nose, which narrows as it rises above the cave into the summit ridge of the cliff, has two facets: the North Face, which lies above and to the left of the

Ogof; and the West Wall, an area of steep grooves and overhangs between the Ogof and the Great Slab to the right. Prominent on the right edge of the Nose is a partly grassy ledge, Sunset Ledge, some 60 metres above the screes, which is visited by many routes in this section.

The cliff is reached from the lakes by unremitting torment up the obvious worn paths in the scree.

In summer, the Great Stone Shoot provides a simple, if long and tiring, descent route for climbs which reach the top of the cliff. It lies around 200 metres to the right as one exits the final ridge and is identifiable by an old fence at its top. The best descent bears to the left. Alternatively, mountaineers climbing with sacks can make a more pleasant descent via the ridge above Clogwyn y Cysgod directly to the track leading to the parking-area. A separate descent is available for those climbs finishing near Sunset Ledge (see the West Wall section for details, page 76).

Eastern Section

This consists of two appropriately-named gullies, *Black* on the left and *Green* on the right, together with their enclosing buttresses. All of the routes in this section finish near the top of *Green Gully* and from there it is but an easy scramble to the foot of *Artist's Climb*, which offers a pleasant continuation to the top of the crag. Alternatively, descent can be made via a diagonal path into the large easy couloir to the right (facing out).

The wide, broken, and vegetated **Heather Rib** marks the beginning of the climbing on the face. What climbing exists is punctuated by plenty of laborious rambling in heather. To the right again, and taking the sharp rib bounding the left edge of *Black Gully*, is a much better route.

★Sunset Rib   99 metres   Difficult   (1913)
A good natural line which, if combined with *Artist's Climb*, provides a pleasant way to the summit without the risk of encountering crowds, save on the final arête (shared with *Outside Edge Route*). The route is rather well worn and extra care should be taken in places, particularly at the short wall above the notch on pitch 2. Start at the foot of the sharp rib.
1 27m. Climb the rib to a large heather ledge which runs left into the depression between the rib and Heather Rib.
2 24m. Traverse right along a narrow ledge until good holds can be followed up and slightly left to a ledge; then go back up right, awkwardly and with care, to some spikes. Continue just left of the crest to a larger notch and good spike belays.
3 18m. Climb easily up heather ledges to reach a point overlooking *Black Gully* just above its dividing rib.
4 18m. Continue pleasantly up just right of the knife-edge to a huge belay on the crest again.
5 12m. Go easily on to the top of *Black Gully*.

Black Gully   70 metres   Very Difficult   (6.9.33)

The left-hand of the two gullies, with a cave near the bottom, which is full of the usual gully contents. Start about 30 metres up, where the gully narrows.

1 15m. Climb the first step on the right; then continue up the groove to belay in the cave.
2 12m. Follow the narrow chimney and then move up to a rib that divides the gully.
3 34m. Climb the right-hand branch to a terrace and follow this to a groove. Ascend the groove; then easier gully-climbing leads to a belay.
4 9m. Scramble to the top.

Black Gully   Winter   III
The lower sections can be hard if not banked out.

It is possible to escape from the gully at the top of the dividing rib on pitch 3 by traversing left to join *Sunset Rib* in the middle of that climb's pitch 3, which is followed to the top.

★Nirvana Wall   94 metres   Severe   (22.8.25)

A good route, taking a line up the left wall of the buttress between *Black* and *Green Gullies*. Start about 10 metres below the first step of *Black Gully*.

1 15m. Gain the heather ledges on the wall of the gully and go up over these to belay beside a large flake level with the cave in the gully.
2 12m. Climb to a ledge on the right; then follow the slanting groove back leftwards to a large pinnacle.
3 18m. Climb up left over ledges to below the obvious nose in the centre of the buttress. Gain the grassy ledge above and climb left into a groove, which leads up right to a stance beneath a bulge.
4 12m. A recess splits the bulge. Gain the recess with difficulty on elusive holds and continue to ledges and a terrace.
5 37m. Climb the right-hand wall of the next section until scrambling leads to the top of *Green Gully*.

Green Gully   72 metres   Hard Very Severe   (13.6.70)

Perhaps the hardest route of its type in Wales. It is well protected but normally very wet and slimy. Start by scrambling up to the chimney at the start of the gully proper.

1 30m. Climb the chimney or the groove to the left; then continue more easily up the gully bed to belay at the narrows.
2 30m. 5a. Climb to a bulge at 6 metres, where the gully closes to a crack. Negotiate this and follow the crack above with difficulty to a resting-place. Move up a little; then climb the slabby wall and grass above leading to a large flake belay at the end of the Ogof Terrace.
3 12m. Move up into a niche and step onto the right wall; then climb up and left on good holds to a grassy finish.

Craig Fawr

1 Engineers' Climb   VD
2 Bankers' Buttress S
3 L.M.H.   M

Craig yr Ogof

4 Sunset Rib   D
5 Black Gully   III
6 Nirvana Wall   S
7 Green Gully   HVS
8 Artist's Climb D
9 Brutus   E2
10 Ogof Direct   E1
11 Desfinado   HVS

The West Wall

1	Ogof Direct	E1
2	Oblique Route	S
3	Desifinado	HVS
4	Crucible	HVS
5	Codswallop	E2
6	Jabberwocky	E2
7	Bourdillon's Climb	E4
8	Penates	HVS
9	Bandersnatch	E3
10	Eureka	E1

The Nose of Craig yr Ogof

The Great Slab

11	Outside Edge Route	VD
12	Ordinary Route	D
13	Direct Route	VD
14	Kirkus's Route	VS
15	Kirkus's Direct	HVS
16	Aquarius	VS
17	Upper Slab Climb	S
18	West Arête	VS

Sunset Ledge

Ogof Terrace

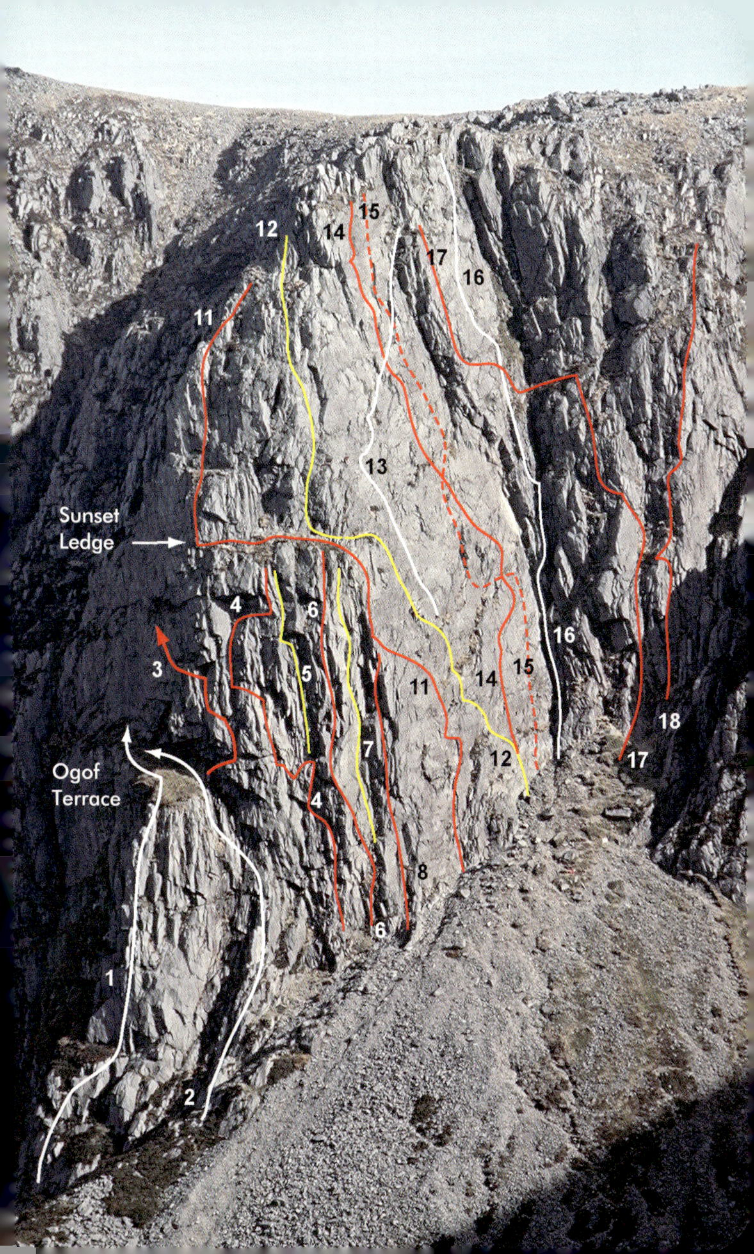

Sunset Ledge
Ogof Terrace
1
2
3
4
5
6
7
8
11
12
13
14
15
16
17
18

Penates (HVS), Craig yr Ogof
Climber: Nigel Coe   Photo: Don Sargeant

Atrocity Run   Winter V
Green Gully provides a hard winter route, with the second pitch being the crux as in summer. Finish up *Artist's Climb*.

The next climb goes up to the final ridge of Craig yr Ogof and starts some distance above the finishes of the previous routes.

Artist's Climb   44 metres   Difficult   (4.25)
Not a route worth seeking out for itself, but a good continuation to the preceding routes allowing one to reach the summit ridge. The final section is shared with *Ordinary Route* and *Outside Edge Route*, which arrive at the other side of the nose. The start is reached by a scramble up from the top of *Green Gully*. Gain and climb a 6-metre crack behind a pinnacle some 12 metres up from the top of the gully; then continue across a terrace and go up onto another terrace close under the ridge. Traverse along this second terrace to a V-chimney near its right-hand end.
1 14m. Climb the chimney to the ridge.
2 30m. Move right onto the crest of the ridge, climb easily to the step in the ridge above, and cross it to some large spikes.
Scrambling on the summit ridge remains.

Ogof Nose – North Face

The main substance of this face is the upper wall above the Ogof Terrace, which harbours a number of shallow grooves that slant slightly leftwards. The grooves are rather blank and incut holds are uncommon, but the rock itself is firm and rough. Unfortunately, the area takes a lot of drainage and faces north, so takes a long time to dry out and is less frequently in condition than the rest of the cliff. In wet conditions the routes will be found harder than the grades would suggest.

The lower tier of the face, below the Ogof Terrace, is mostly vegetated to the left and easy-angled to the right. The first route, which traverses the upper part of the wall, starts above the lower tier.

Jones's Traverse   63 metres   Very Severe   (26.5.58)
The easiest climb on the upper wall takes the obvious rightward-trending line of ledges from the top of *Green Gully* to Sunset Ledge. Pleasant climbing in a good position in the middle of the steep wall makes it worth doing in good conditions. Start in the bay at the top of *Green Gully*.
1 15m. Go easily across heather ledges to a large block belay.
2 18m. 4b. Continue along the ledges to reach a corner. Move across to follow a sloping ledge and more heather to another corner; then step down to belay at a triangular ledge.
3 15m. 4c. Move up and round the edge, and ascend a short wall to a good ledge. Follow a descending traverse to the grassy ledge at the top of pitch 4 of *Ogof Direct*.
4 15m. 4c. Climb up and right, and go across under the overhang. After a step right, pleasant slabs lead diagonally up right to Sunset Ledge.

The next route begins up the impressive crack in the right wall of *Green Gully* and then trends rightwards up the steep walls of the upper tier.

★**Brutus**   78 metres   E2   (30.5.66)
A fine varied route. A strenuous crack on the first pitch leads to steep wall-climbing above. Start at the top of the first pitch of *Green Gully*.
1 21m. 5a. Gain the grassy ledge below the steep crack in the right wall of the gully. Climb the crack past two bulges to a small grassy bay.
2 15m. 4a. Follow the open chimney at the back of the bay to Ogof Terrace. Move rightwards along this for 8 metres to belay at a flake at the foot of a shallow groove.
3 18m. 5c. Start up the groove; then move right onto the arête. Climb this to a resting-place at 12 metres; then continue slightly left to gain the ledges of *Jones's Traverse*. Move up left to a stance.
4 24m. 4c. Climb up for a couple of metres and step right onto a sloping ledge. Climb the leaning groove on the right to reach another ledge at 12 metres. Move right; then go up to the right on good holds to belay on a large ledge.

The ledge below the final pitch of *Outside Edge Route* is easily reached around to the right.

The area immediately to the right of *Green Gully* in the lower tier is particularly vegetated and wet. Further right again, and directly below the cave, is a fine grey rib.

★★**Ogof Direct**   113 metres   E1   (5.7.52)
A very good route, which follows the relatively easy rib to the Ogof Terrace and then the awkward grooves left of the cave. Start about 6 metres up the field of rushes on the left of the rib. This can be reached directly or from the screes on the right via a heather ledge.
1 11m. Move along the ledge above on the right into a small corner. Climb the left wall of the corner and step right onto the ledge at the top.
2 37m. 4b. Step right onto the rib and follow it to a grassy ledge below two short corners. Climb either corner (the right is easier) to another ledge. Step back left onto the main rib and ascend this to the cave. Belay well back.
3 21m. Cross the terrace to a peg belay just to the left of the groove on the left-hand side of the cave.
4 23m. 5c. Move up rightwards into the groove and climb it to a small ledge at 12 metres. Move up right with difficulty to a sloping ledge and continue up right in a fine position to better holds, which are followed to a grassy ledge below another, smaller overhang.
5 21m. 5a. Continue up the slanting groove above to a ledge at 8 metres. Move right and climb another groove to easier rocks leading up to the ledge below the final pitch of *Outside Edge Route*.

Oblique Route   100 metres   Severe   (4.8.46)
A poor and rambling route, which takes an obvious line into the right-hand side of the cave, and then crosses *The Ogof Traverse* to finish up *Green Gully*. The climbing up to the cave takes one of the main drainage lines from the Ogof Terrace. Start at a rib composed of huge blocks on the right-hand side of the steep open gully which descends from the right-hand end of the cave.
1 Climb the rib to where it peters out in loose rock; then traverse left across the gully to a quartz ledge. Climb the slabby left wall of the gully into the cave.
2 27m. Cross the terrace to the left-hand side of the cave. Move up onto the continuation of the ledge and follow it leftwards to a flake belay at the foot of a shallow groove at the end of pitch 3 of *Brutus*.
3 24m. Continue along the ledge until it again disappears. Step down and across the top of a chimney to gain the continuation of the terrace. Follow this to a large flake belay in *Green Gully*.
4 12m. Move up into a niche, step onto the right wall, and then climb up and left on good holds to a grassy finish.

★**Desifinado**   100 metres   Hard Very Severe   (4.10.64)
A steep, sustained, and exposed route, which starts on the North Face and moves through the overhangs on the right of the cave to reach *Crucible* on the West Wall, and then returns leftwards to finish up *Ogof Direct*.
1 37m. *Oblique Route* pitch 1.
2 18m. 5a. Traverse right out of the cave in an exciting position between two sets of overhangs into a bottomless corner. Move up onto a ledge on the right and climb straight up into the bottom of the large overhang-capped corner of *Crucible*.
3 24m. 5a. Step left round the block and climb diagonally left to a niche below a large square-cut overhang. Move out left and climb a diagonal crack until a traverse left can be made to the grassy ledges at the top of pitch 4 of *Ogof Direct*.
4 21m. 5a. *Ogof Direct* pitch 5.
Variation
3a 27m. E1. Move left above the block and follow the groove above. Instead of going right as for *Crucible*, continue straight up, passing a square-cut overhang on its right, and then move left round a second overhang to a ledge. Traverse left again to join pitch 3 of the original route.

Ogof Nose – West Wall

Again, this takes on something of a two-tier structure: above the level of the Ogof is a complex area of grooves and overhangs between the Nose and the Great Slab; below, the rock is relatively easy-angled and prone to seepage.

There are so many features on this section of the crag that distinguishing them apart appears at first sight to be impossible. Sunset Ledge is the grassy terrace that is situated at about two-thirds height on the right-hand side of the face and running to the right arête. In the centre of the upper wall is a large corner capped by a large square-cut overhang. This corner leads from the right-hand side of the Ogof to just below the left-hand end of Sunset Ledge and is taken by the final pitch of *Crucible*. To the right of the Ogof are a series of smooth grooves which form the highlights of most of the routes hereabouts. The obvious large rock-scar to the right of the large corner is visited by *Eureka*. The central groove capped by a triangular roof is taken by *Codswallop*. See page 72b for diagram.

Most of the routes are worth doing and some are of exceptional quality in a fine position. The rock is basically sound but there are a surprising number of insecure blocks and spikes about. The wall dries out much faster than the north side of the Nose and any dampness may indeed increase the difficulties substantially on some routes.

All of the routes finish on Sunset Ledge, from which a descent is usually made by reversing the first pitch and a half of *Ordinary Route* (page 80.) This is straightforward and obvious.

★Eureka   72 metres   E1   (27.8.66)
A worthwhile eliminate through *Crucible* with two short hard sections. Start as for *Oblique Route*, at the rib to the right of the open gully.
1 18m. Climb the rib of pitch 1 of *Oblique Route* to belay where that route traverses left across the gully.
2 27m. 5b. Go over a bulge and climb up rightwards to the perched block below the corner on the second pitch of *Crucible*. Move left to a weakness in the overhangs and climb straight through this to the sloping ledge on *Crucible*. Continue up a groove until it is possible to step left to a small stance.
3 27m. 5b. Move down right into a groove and climb it to reach a short diagonal crack on the right, which leads onto the right arête; then continue more easily to the ledge below the final slabby groove of *Crucible*. Climb the groove to Sunset Ledge.

Bandersnatch   64 metres   E3   (15.6.82)
A direct line between *Eureka* and *Codswallop*, following the groove which is crossed by *Eureka*'s third pitch. Some hard climbing with poor rock and dubious protection. Scramble up to overhangs at 12 metres to start. Above here a smooth rib leads to the perched block to which *Crucible*'s pitch 2 descends.
1 24m. 5a. Move up right and go through the overhangs to gain a slabby rib via a leftward-slanting groove. Follow the rib via shallow grooves to reach the perched block. Climb up and right to the first stance of *Crucible*.
2 40m. 5c. Climb the blank groove above the left end of the ledge, via the left wall, to gain a deeper groove. Follow this to join *Crucible* under the overhang. Move right into a niche and go right again to a slabby groove. Follow this to Sunset Ledge (as for *Crucible*).

To the right, the base of the crag steps back into a confusing area of ribs and grooves. The next two routes begin to the right-hand side of this area, at a pair of grooves.

★**Codswallop** 70 metres E2 (9.6.68)
A good route, taking the obvious large central groove of the upper wall. Start as for *Crucible*.
1 30m. 5a. Climb the left-hand of the two grooves until level with the triangular overhang at 18 metres; then continue direct to gain the stance below the central groove.
2 40m. 5b. Ascend the groove to a small overhang; then move up left to gain a crack. Climb this to a small ledge and follow the left wall of the groove past the left side of the main overhang. Traverse right into an easy groove, which leads to Sunset Ledge.

★★**Crucible** 91 metres Hard Very Severe (1.6.63)
A classic route, taking the easiest line hereabouts. It crosses the wall diagonally left to reach the largest groove and then turns the large overhang high on the wall on the right. Start about 12 metres left of the edge of the Great Slab, on the right-hand side of the depression below the twin grooves.
1 30m. 4c. Climb the left-hand of the twin grooves to a small overhang, step right and climb the other groove, and then move back left to a large triangular overhang at 18 metres. Climb another groove on the left for a couple of metres; then step right above the roof and follow an easier line diagonally rightwards to a stance.
2 24m. 5b. Move down leftwards onto a large perched block. Climb the corner above past an overhang (peg) and go up left to gain a sloping ledge. Step left around the rib into a groove; then go down and left again to gain a sloping gangway, which leads leftwards to the foot of the large corner. Climb the corner a short way to a small stance beside a large block.
3 37m. 5a. From the top of the block, step left and climb another groove and its right-hand rib until it is possible to regain the main corner. Continue up past a bulge to a small ledge. Traverse right across the slab and then climb delicately up to the roof. Move right into a niche and go right again to a slabby groove, which leads to Sunset Ledge.
Variation
The original version of this route took the left-hand groove direct to the overhang at 18 metres, the second pitch as described to the sloping ledge, and then a higher line into the main corner, leading direct to the normal finish. This is harder than the route as described.

★★**Jabberwocky** 64 metres E2 (18.5.70)
A great Welsh mountain route: enjoyable airy climbing up the grooved arête to the right of *Codswallop*. Start below the arête in a grassy groove, about 6 metres left of the edge of the Great Slab.
1 30m. 5a. Climb the groove to a grassy ledge. Move up left onto the arête and follow its right edge by the easiest line to a sloping stance beneath the steep upper wall.

2 34m. 5c. Move out left from under the small roof to gain a spike; then go back up right into the main groove. Climb this with difficulty past a peg, and move out left to gain an exposed gangway. Follow the gangway easily up left until it is possible to move right across a slab in a fine position to gain the arête on the right. Move right into a shallow groove, which leads to Sunset Ledge.

Bourdillon's Climb 64 metres E4 (26.5.56)
The jagged groove in the smooth wall to the right of *Jabberwocky* gives a taxing climb with poor protection and friable rock. Start as for *Jabberwocky*, in a grassy groove 6 metres left of the edge of the Great Slab.
1 37m. 5a. Follow the groove past ledges to a bulge at 15 metres. Traverse out left onto the slab and climb back rightwards up the slab into the corner. Climb the corner, and move right at the top onto a sloping ledge.
2 27m. 6a. Move left and climb the subsidiary corner and the flake above to a resting-place. Follow the groove with continuing difficulty to a niche; then traverse left to join the easy finishing-groove of *Jabberwocky*.

Penates 48 metres Hard Very Severe (18.5.63)
A short but interesting climb based on the arête between the West Face and the Great Slab. Start at a short slab just left of the edge of the Great Slab.
1 30m. 5a. Climb the slab, then the short wall above to gain the arête. Climb the arête to a ledge at 18 metres where the wall steepens. Step left onto the wall and climb it with difficulty to a ledge; then follow a groove to a perched block.
2 18m. 5a. Climb the corner above the block to the ledge at the top of pitch 1 of *Bourdillon's Climb*. Gain the steep crack on the right and follow it for 5 metres until it is possible to move out right to a ledge on *Outside Edge Route*, which is followed to the stance on Sunset Ledge.

★The Ogof Traverse 123 metres Hard Very Severe (10.64)
A pleasant collection of pitches traversing both walls of the Nose.
1 30m. 5a. *Penates* pitch 1.
2 24m. 4c. Climb the corner above the block to the ledge at the top of pitch 1 of *Bourdillon's Climb*. From the left-hand end of the ledge, move down until a line of holds leads left to the stance of *Jabberwocky*. Step down left again and go round to the stance of *Crucible*.
3 24m. 5b. *Crucible* pitch 2.
4 24m. 5a. *Desifinado* pitch 3.
5 21m. 5a *Ogof Direct* pitch 5.
An alternative to the last pitch is to reverse pitches 3, 2, and 1 of *Jones's Traverse*.

The Great Slab

This fine slab of rock reaches up the west side of Craig yr Ogof for some 100 metres to the summit ridge. Having good rock and a sunny aspect, it is a popular resort for the lower-grade climber. All the routes described are worth doing and there are many other possibilities as well – the slab is climbable virtually anywhere. However, there are few obvious landmarks once one is on a route, and on some it is quite easy to lose the line.

About 15 metres up the centre of the main slab is a depression containing grassy ledges which reach out to the left edge of the slab. These are visited by *Ordinary Route*, which then takes a rising leftward line across to Sunset Ledge to finish up the prow of the crag.

The main slab to the right of *Ordinary Route* is divided by three breaks running diagonally right. Theses are not very apparent in some lights and tend to disappear altogether when one is actually on the slab. The first consists of two grassy rakes about 3 metres apart which rise from the ledges on *Ordinary Route*. The lower of these two ends at the top of the first pitch of *Kirkus's Route* and the upper steepens into the small corner taken by both of the *Kirkus's Route* variations. The middle break connects Sunset Ledge with the top of pitch 2 of *Kirkus's Route*, and the upper break provides the unpleasant finish for *Direct Route*, which gains it via the centre of the slab.

High on the right of the main slab, and separated from it by a corner which runs the full height of the crag, is the Upper Slab.

Diagram page 72c.

★★**Outside Edge Route**   136 metres   Very Difficult   (14.7.31)
A Welsh mountain classic, taking a good line up the left edge of the slab with an exposed finish above the nose of the crag. Start 6 metres right of the edge of the slab, below a large, semi-detached block.
1 21m. Climb a rightward-trending groove to gain the block by its right edge.
2 24m. Move up steeply to the next ledge and then make a fine ascending traverse across the wall to the left arête. Follow this to ledges.
3 12m. Continue up for 6 metres to Sunset Ledge and move left to belay at its left-hand end, beyond the open groove of *Ordinary Route*.
4 15m. Move leftwards round a couple of ribs into a groove, and climb it to a large grassy ledge in a fine position on the brow of the buttress.
5 24m. Move up; then go left and climb a wide crack in a corner. Follow this until it is possible to step left onto the rib, which leads more easily to a junction with *Artist's Climb* and *Ordinary Route*.
6 30m. Easy climbing in a good position leads up the ridge to the top.
Direct Start
1a 21m. Severe. This is only a little harder than the original line, starting at the extreme left-hand edge of the slab and climbing up slightly rightwards to the left side of the block at the top of the first pitch of the normal route.

The next four routes all start at the same place: a pedestal 6 metres above the scree and some 12 metres left of the right-hand corner of the slab. The top of this pedestal is approximately level with the block on *Outside Edge Route*.

★★Ordinary Route   109 metres   Difficult   (4.4.26)

The original route of the slab, following a rising leftward line of ledges to Sunset Ledge and taking the open groove and slabs above. Beware of parties descending from routes on the West Wall.

1 27m. Climb the short polished wall on the right; then follow easy ledges up leftwards to belay below a broken groove.
2 21m. Continue diagonally left to the edge of the slab and move up to Sunset Ledge. Go along the ledge for 5 metres to belay below an open groove.
3 24m. Follow the groove to a short slab at 12 metres, and climb this and the nose above to belay on a ledge where the angle eases.
4 37m. Go round to the left, and climb easily at first before crossing the step in the ridge above to reach large spikes. Scramble up the summit ridge.

Variations

Inside Variation   30 metres   Difficult
From the top of pitch 1, follow the broken groove above past a stance eventually to rejoin the parent route at the short slab on pitch 3.

Inside Finish   30 metres   Very Difficult
From the foot of the short slab on pitch 3, traverse right to join *Direct Route*. Follow this for a short way; then climb the steep exposed crack above, moving left when the angle eases, to the top of the cliff.

Direct Route   108 metres   Very Difficult   (1927)

A good route, but marred by the finish, which is often covered with stones and earth. It takes a direct line up the left-hand side of the main slab to reach the highest of the three breaks. This is followed up rightwards to a finish in the right-hand corner of the slab.

1 30m. Climb *Ordinary Route* pitch 1, but then continue 3 metres up the broken groove taken by *Inside Variation* to a stance.
2 24m. Ignoring the leftward-trending break of *Inside Variation*, climb straight up for 8 metres to another ledge, move awkwardly up right, and then traverse left for 5 metres to gain a shallow groove at the left-hand end of a small line of overhangs. Follow the groove for a few metres and then traverse right to ledges on the middle break of the slab.
3 24m. Go up, trending slightly left to a grassy ledge below two short grooves. Start up the left-hand groove; then gain the other groove and follow it to the left end of another line of small overhangs. Move up and left and then back right to a good ledge at the start of the upper break.
4 30m. Carefully follow the break up right into the corner. Climb this, with disheartening protection, past a large ledge, to finish up the slab on the left of the corner. Great care should be taken not to knock stones down onto parties below.

Central Variant   96 metres   Hard Very Severe   (13.4.52)

An artificial but worthwhile route, which moves left from *Kirkus's Route* to find a more direct line up the middle of the slab.

1 27m. 4c. *Kirkus's Route* pitch 1; or *Kirkus's Direct* pitch 1 (5a).

Crucible (HVS), Craig yr Ogof
Climbers: unknown   Photo: Don Sargeant

Climber: Pat Cocks   Photo: Martin Whitaker

Kirkus's Route (VS), Craig yr Ogof
Climber: Tim Cairns   Photo: Don Sargeant

2 21m. 5a. Go easily up and left to gain the small corner at the end of the upper of the two rakes which run up from *Ordinary Route*. Climb the corner for 3 metres to a small spike; then traverse left above the small overhangs and continue up leftwards to reach the middle break at the top of pitch 2 of *Direct Route*.
3 24m. *Direct Route* pitch 3.
4 24m. 5a. Move up left to a small overhang and climb the thin crack on its left. Continue up the groove and slab above to another overhang, which is taken by the crack on its right. Easy climbing leads to the top.

★★★Kirkus's Route   97 metres   Very Severe   (31.5.31)
An elegant slab climb with a modern feel giving sustained climbing throughout. The best climb here. It takes a nearly direct line up the the slab about 10 metres from the right-hand corner, and finishes just above the step in the summit ridge. Many minor variations are possible with no change in grade. Start at the pedestal.
1 27m. 4c. Climb the short polished wall as for *Ordinary Route* to gain some ledges; then move up to the forked diagonal crack above. Climb the crack, following the right-hand branch round a corner into a niche. Continue more steeply to a stance on blocks.
2 21m. 4b. Step right and climb a depression leading up to the right. Step left into a leftward-leaning groove and follow it to belay on the middle break.
3 15m. 4c. Climb the smooth slab above via the vague weakness in its centre over several small overlaps to reach a stance on *Direct Route*.
4 24m. 4c. Climb diagonally leftwards over a protruding block to large holds below a nose of rock. Swing rightwards until holds above the overlap lead up leftwards to the summit ridge.
Variation Starts
It is possible to climb the wet slab of *Kirkus's Direct* to the overhang and then traverse left to gain the diagonal crack. One can also climb direct to the start of the crack through the steep wall. Both alternatives are similar in grade to the normal way.

★★Kirkus's Direct   94 metres   Hard Very Severe   (1951)
A good climb with some exciting, delicate sections, and the crux at the very top of the climb. Start 5 metres from the right-hand corner of the slab.
1 27m. 5a. Climb the wet slab to an overhang, and up round it to the foot of a shallow groove which leans to the right. Follow this awkwardly to a sentry-box at its top. Traverse leftwards past flakes and step down to the stance at the top of pitch 1 of *Kirkus's Route*.
2 24m. 4c. Go easily up and left to gain the small corner at the end of the upper of the two rakes which run up from *Ordinary Route*, as for *Central Variant*. Climb the corner for 3 metres to a small spike on the rib; then step right onto the rib. Continue up the thin crack above until it is possible to move left to an easy groove. Follow this rightwards to join *Kirkus's Route* near the top of its second pitch. Belay as for that route.

3 43m. 5b. Move right into the corner on the right of the slab and follow it to a small overhang. Climb the crack on the left to a mossy area; then step left and continue directly up the slab about 3 metres from the corner to reach the upper break in the slab and a junction with *Direct Route*. Continue straight up the slim groove in the final slab.

Upper Slab and South-West Buttress

Aquarius 100 metres Very Severe (20.3.66)
A reasonable climb, but the first pitches are always wet, even in a good summer. If very wet they may well be harder than the grade suggests. Start below the corner at the right-hand end of The Great Slab.
1 18m. 5a. Go up to the base of the corner and climb its left wall for about 5 metres until it is possible to move right to join the corner itself. Follow the corner past a niche to gain a short slab on the right. Climb the shallow groove on the left of the slab and then step left to belay on a small ledge.
2 24m. 4c. Move right into the bed of the gully and follow it to where it narrows and steepens. Step left and climb the groove to a grassy ledge, and continue up the slab on the left to a ledge.
3 18m. Continue up the slab to a grassy area on the right below the main part of the Upper Slab.
4 40m. 4c. Go up and left across the slab. Continue straight up past a line of overhangs near the top to finish easily.

Aquarian Wall Winter V
The best winter route here. Follow the summer line of *Aquarius* with some variations in the upper section according to conditions.

Kangies Crawl 60 metres Very Severe (2.10.62)
This route covers very similar ground to the next route and takes a line of grooves up the buttress. Start at the lowest point of the South-West Buttress.
1 18m. Climb the left wall of a groove to belay on a large ledge.
2 12m. Start up the left corner of the ledge for 6 metres; then traverse right to the continuation of the starting-line.
3 12m. Move round to the right onto a steep wall and go up for 6 metres to a ledge. Continue up to a belay below an overhang.
4 18m. Move left across a short wall and left again to the arête. Climb this to the summit fields.

★Upper Slab Climb 116 metres Severe (2.8.31)
A wandering route, which finds a fine exposed finish. Start at a grassy groove just right of an obvious double overhang about 12 metres right of the corner at the right-hand end of The Great Slab.
1 21m. Ascend the groove to a niche; then climb its left wall until the groove can be regained and followed to a large grassy ledge.
2 37m. Climb the corner on the left for 6 metres, move left, and go up the slab to a small ledge in a corner below an overhang. Traverse left and climb the narrowing slab to heather ledges and a belay on the left.

3 15m. Follow the grassy rake down to the left to join *Aquarius*. Climb the corner and steep grass to a small grassy ledge.
4 43m. Go down to a narrow ledge above the overhang on the slab and follow it out left until near the edge. Climb up and slightly right to gain a shallow groove, which leads up left to a ledge overlooking The Great Slab. Traverse back right onto the Upper Slab and go diagonally right to the top.

White Snake Winter V
The lower half of *Upper Slab Climb* is linked to the upper part of *West Arête* via a difficult traverse.

West Arête 63 metres Very Severe (23.5.70)
A clean and attractive climb up the right-hand arête of South-West Buttress. Start below the arête, in the left-hand of three grassy grooves.
1 21m. 4c. Climb the groove for 6 metres until level with the base of a crack in the left wall. Gain the crack and follow it to the large ledge at the top of pitch 1 of *Upper Slab Climb*.
2 15m. 4c. Continue up the smooth groove just left of the arête to gain a sloping ledge.
3 27m. 4c. Climb the steep groove above the stance for 3 metres; then step left into a crack on the arête. Climb up and left to a shallow depression, which leads in a fine position to the top.

Rib and Tower 135 metres Difficult (22.7.36)
A poor, rambling, and vegetated route, taking a line up the left wall of Amphitheatre Gully. Start about 15 metres below and to the right of *West Arête*, at the foot of a rib just left of Amphitheatre Gully. Climb the rib to a grassy ledge at 27 metres. Take the next section slightly on the left for 18 metres. Follow the rib again for 15 metres to a large terrace. Stroll along this for 30 metres to the foot of some grassy ribs converging on a grassy tower about 30 metres above. Climb the rightmost rib to the tower and pass this easily on the right.

Amphitheatre Gully (130 metres) gives a winter grade 1. In summer it is wet, and not recommended as a means of descent except to those who have a penchant for hospital food.

Amphitheatre Buttress

This is the huge sprawling mass right of Amphitheatre Gully. Despite its size it is not as good as its namesake on Craig yr Ysfa, offering only isolated pitches with much vegetation in between.

Original Route 150 metres Difficult (4.25)
Best avoided, although some more interesting rock does appear at the finish. Start on the left of the buttress, near the gully. Climb short slabby buttresses and rather a lot of heather for 60 metres to an extensive field. At the far end of the field the buttress narrows, and a fine arête leads to the top.

Gotogo 40 metres Very Severe (23.5.70)
A vegetated route up the slabby lower section of the buttress right of *Original Route*. Start at a slabby groove at the lowest point of the buttress. Climb the groove to a small overhang; then go diagonally left to a stance below another overhang. Move back right and climb the obvious groove until it is possible to step left onto the rib. Follow this to a large terrace.

High up in the Great Stone Shoot, and well seen during descent, is a short steep tower in the right wall of Amphitheatre Buttress; this gives three routes.

Jericho 57 metres Difficult (4.6.49)
The steep wall is avoided. The climbing is rather poor and some of the rock dubious. Start in the gully at the foot of the chimney, down and to the left of the wall.
1 9m. Climb the chimney to a belay on the left.
2 30m. Move back right to beneath the wall and climb up trending right to a belay on top of a pyramid of blocks.
3 18m. Climb to a ledge above; then move round the edge to the right and ascend consecutive cracks to the top.

★Tower of Strength 34 metres Very Severe 4c (3.9.55)
Good steep climbing up the obvious crack and chimney in the centre of the tower. Start just left of a yellow rock scar on the ledges above the gully and below the chimney. Climb the cracked wall to the foot of the steep crack. Ascend the crack to the foot of the chimney, which is climbed to the top via a ledge.
The route originally avoided the central crack by climbing the right arête (Severe).

Afterthought 37 metres Severe (23.7.67)
The right-hand side of the tower. Start just right of the yellow rock-scar at the foot of the curving groove. Gain the groove from the right and follow it to a ledge at 18 metres. Move up left to go through the overlap; then traverse 3 metres right to an easy groove, which is climbed to the top.

The Great Stone Shoot (130 metres) can give a pleasant winter grade I amidst impressive scenery.

The Widow of the Web 200 metres *Winter* IV
A line in five pitches based on the most obvious icefalls to the right of the Great Stone Shoot.

Clogwyn y Cysgod The Shade Cliff OS Ref 512 501
This brooding and vegetated cliff on the western arm of Cwm Silyn is overshadowed by its more illustrious twin to the north-east, and is separated from the Great Stone Shoot by a wide expanse of easy ground. The dampness and vegetation conspire to render it a most unattractive playground in the summer months. A good freeze, however, greatly enhances the appeal.

The cliff is bounded on the left by *Four-Pitch Gully*, which faces Craig yr Ogof and is well viewed from the Great Slab, though not from the floor of the cwm. To the right of the gully, the first buttress of the cliff has a series of large overhangs at half height. Below the overhangs it is broken by large grassy terraces, except to the right where continuous rock leads to the indefinite groove passing the overhangs on their right. Right again is a wide vegetated weakness and another broken buttress.

In the centre of the cliff is an amphitheatre, out of which rises a dark ravine, *The Little Kitchen*. The grassy *Kitchen Rake* leads up left from the amphitheatre and is separated from *The Little Kitchen* by the steep rib taken by *Sideline*. To the right of *The Little Kitchen* and beyond another very vegetated buttress is an impressive deep and dripping cleft, *Bedrock Gully*, the right wall of which is the steep and narrow *Flintstone Rib*. Beyond this feature the cliff falls back into a large vegetated depression. The last climbing on the cliff lies on the rather indistinct buttress to the right of this depression.

The approach from the lakes up the screes on the right-hand side of the cwm is obvious if tiring. Descent is best made (carefully) via *Kitchen Rake*, which finishes near the top of *Four-Pitch Gully*.

Four-Pitch Gully   93 metres   Difficult   (9.11)
This gully slants from left to right at the left edge of the cliff, and finishes near the top of *The Kitchen Rake* and *The Little Kitchen*. There is much loose scree in its bed. Start below the gully, slightly right of its main line.
1 15m. Climb a little chimney and go on past a block until a steep grassy ledge leads to a belay.
2 27m. Follow the scree to an impressive cave.
3 27m. Exit from the cave via a tight hole and go up the left wall above. Belay beneath a loose wall.
4 24m. Climb the wall, then broken ground, to a final steep, vegetated wall reaching the top.

Four-Pitch Gully   Winter   II/III
Follow the summer line.

Eyrie   98 metres   Hard Very Severe   (10.65)
A vegetated and worrying scramble over terraces leads to the indefinite groove on the right of the conspicuous overhangs on the left side of the cliff. The overhangs are turned by the crack on their left. Some impressive scenery. Start directly below the overhangs.
1 50m. Awkward and unnerving climbing on vegetation leads up to the groove on the right of the overhangs.
2 30m. Climb the groove to the first roof; then traverse diagonally left and climb the crack on its left side to a belay.
3 18m. Climb straight up for 6 metres; then trend left to the top.

Atropos   128 metres   Hard Very Severe   (20.3.66)
A steep wall rises leftwards to the right of *Eyrie*, giving access to an exposed finish above the overhangs.

86 Cwm Silyn

1 50m. Climb a dirty gully for 15 metres until an obvious gangway with a crack at its back leads up to the left. Follow this to a small pinnacle.
2 30m. Ascend the steep wall above the pinnacle and gain a shallow groove. Climb the groove and traverse left at the top to an obvious spike belay.
3 30m. From the top of the spike, step awkwardly onto the arête on the left. Climb the arête to the roof and then a bottomless groove on the left. Trend left along an obvious traverse to join *Eyrie* at its second stance.
4 18m. *Eyrie* pitch 3.

Beyond the vague gully at the start of *Atropos* is a broken buttress with no routes. This is bounded on the right by the easy watercourse which leads up into the amphitheatre below *The Little Kitchen*. Running up left from the amphitheatre is the **The Kitchen Rake**, which is only a walk apart from a 5-metre wall a short way up. **The Little Kitchen** (19.4.35) itself contains a pitch of piled boulders, some of which are loose – not recommended except in winter (II/III).

Between the two is a rib.

Sideline 46 metres   Very Severe   (1962)
Start below the centre of the rib, high up in the amphitheatre. Climb vegetated rocks on the left and then go rightwards up a small slab to gain a grassy chimney-crack. Follow this for a short way; then step round right into a slabby groove. Follow the groove and the shallow chimney above to a stance on the left at 24 metres in the wider grassy chimney. Continue easily up to the summit ridge.

About 60 metres down to the right from the entrance to *The Little Kitchen* is another conspicuous gully, *Bedrock Gully*. **Sweep Wall** (26.3.33) climbs its left arête.

Bedrock Gully 90 metres   Very Difficult   (26.3.33)
This dark, narrow gully is usually very wet indeed and cannot in the slightest respect be recommended as a summer climb – even Menlove Edwards thought it unjustifiable! The left-hand branch is still unclimbed in summer, though in winter this is **Mask of Death** (IV/V); the main right-hand line is IV.

Flintstone Rib   91 metres   Very Severe   (20.10.62)
A loose route taking the prominent rib which bounds *Bedrock Gully* to the right. Start just inside the gully at the foot of the rib.
1 24m. Climb up steep loose rock and grass until it is possible to step right onto the front of the rib below a steep slab. Climb this diagonally rightwards over a bulge on the arête; then traverse left to a small stance overlooking the gully.
2 37m. Climb straight up behind the stance into a groove and step left onto a slab. Go up for a couple of metres and then step back into the groove, which is followed to a large grassy ledge. Move right and go up a chimney to another grassy ledge.
3 30m. Grassy scrambling up the ridge leads to the top.

On the right of *Flintstone Rib* is a shallow, indefinite gully, then a wide vegetated depression. At the right-hand end of this is a steep buttress with a smooth front. The next route follows a groove on the left side of this buttress.

Cysgodian Creep　90 metres　Very Severe　　　　　　　(14.6.70)
Start below the buttress. Gain a grassy rake and follow it to a short wall just below the steep part of the buttress. Surmount the wall; then move left into a slabby groove which slants left. Climb the groove past a bulge to easier climbing and a large grassy ledge at 30 metres. Continue up the break for 12 metres; then follow vegetation to the top.

To the right, the cliff falls back into a confused area of heather terraces and short buttresses; the indefinite **Colin's Gully** (7.6.51) takes a line up here, better in winter (IV).

Craig Cwm Dulyn　Black Lake Hollow Crag　OS Ref 512 501

This small steep crag lies in a pleasant secluded position above Llyn Cwm Dulyn. It offers the only climbing on the northern slopes of Mynydd Craig Goch. The crag is very vegetated and the existing routes have required extensive gardening. Prospective ascensionists should be aware that, owing to lack of traffic, some further cleaning will be needed.

Local legend has it that this lake is connected by a subterranean passageway to Llynnau Cwm Silyn. However, a look at the map shows that the differences in altitude make it unlikely.

The crag is easily accessible and is situated low enough sometimes to be in condition when higher crags are shrouded in mist. Because of the vegetation, however, it remains greasy for long periods, and at least a week of fine weather may be required for the climbs to dry out.

Cwm Dulyn can be reached in around 20 minutes over the moor from Bryn Gwyn, the start of the usual approach to Cwm Silyn. However, the closest public road is the end of the service track for the reservoir at OS Ref 488 498. This track is approached via Nebo and the Caernarfon to Porthmadog road. From the parking-place go through the gate and follow the side of the lake until below the crag – boggy in places. The crag can be reached in around 15 minutes from here, though the top of the *Dulyn Groove* area may take slightly longer.

The summer crag is the lower left of the crags. It juts out from the surrounding hillside and is topped by a hidden meadow. Near its left-hand end is an easy rake. The first outcrop right of the rake consists of a slab with an overhang at the bottom. The crack which splits this is about 18 metres long and Severe. Right again a rib of clean rock, **Ebon Ridge** (50 metres Very Severe), rises from the heather and, if the rock is stuck to religiously, provides some pleasant climbing. The route finishes up an obvious corner above a terrace.

The main wall of the crag rises above the vast, steep, heather-covered slope right of these ribs and can be reached by scrambling 9 metres up the rather slimy and unpleasant gully on the left of the heather slope, until an exit left can be made into the bracken. Steep vegetation then leads up right to the foot of *Dulyn Groove*. The sensible will reach this point by abseiling in to the foot of the corner (extra rope needed).

The crag is terminated by a short steep gully divided into two branches by a narrow heather rib.

The quickest descent from the cliff is the easy rake on the left, though this is not easy to locate from above. The gully mentioned above is not recommended as a means of descent.

Just left of *Dulyn Groove* is another groove with a small retaining wall. Left again is a shorter groove slanting leftwards. This is taken by:

Zip Groove   37 metres   Very Severe   (22.5.70)
An interesting pitch if clean, but still hardly worth the effort. Start in the heather and bracken field immediately below *Dulyn Groove*. Climb shattered blocks about 3 metres left of *Dulyn Groove*; then traverse left to a large spike and, from its top, follow the shallow groove up left for about 12 metres until easier ground is reached, leading to a belay at the top of the crag.

★**The Bodysnatchers**   40 metres   E3 6a   (6.8.88)
The groove left of *Dulyn Groove*. From the blocks, climb the groove past a tricky overlap. Finish up an awkward off-width crack.

★★**Dulyn Groove**   43 metres   E3 5c   (18.10.70)
A fine sustained pitch, at once delicate and strenuous, with an impressive finish. The grade assumes that the route is clean. Start directly below the groove. Follow the groove, awkward at first, to a resting-place at 9 metres. Move up to the bulge above and pass this to another resting-place. Move out onto the slabby left wall and go up it for 3 metres before making a rising traverse to good footholds on the left arête. Step up; then traverse back right into the groove and climb it to a grassy finish.

★**Nordor**   37 metres   E4 5c   (11.5.89)
An exhilarating route, taking the right-hand arête of *Dulyn Groove*. Start as for that route. Climb the first couple of metres of *Dulyn Groove* until a horizontal ledge can be hand-traversed into the middle of the wall. Move up to gain a good sidehold; then go up and right to the arête. Climb the arête for a short way on its right and swing round left to climb a short crack. Pull back right and climb a shallow groove in the arête itself. At the top, step slightly right and pull over the bulge onto the wall above. Climb the wall for a few metres; then move left to gain a good spike and belays just above.

To the right of the arête the wall is very vegetated and forms a short overhanging corner where it meets the longer, lower buttress to its right.

Quest for Corbeau 72 metres   Very Severe   (22.3.52)
The first section of the buttress, to the rock-scar, is quite pleasant and interesting, but after that the route gradually deteriorates into tedious heather scrambling. Start in the gully near the right-hand edge of the crag, where the buttress steepens and a vegetated ledge runs left round to its front.
1 24m. Traverse left along the ledge and round a rib formed by a huge perched block. Go up the crack on the left side of the block for 3 metres; then climb up left into a steep little groove with a tiny overhang formed by a suspect block. Move up to the overhang, swing left onto the rib, and step up to a small ledge just below the rock-scar. Climb a loose but easy shallow groove on the left to the scar; then traverse the scar rising rightwards to ledges.
2 21m. Climb the broken, rightward-trending groove until it is possible to scramble up left to the top of the buttress, where it abuts onto the main crag.
3 27m. Scramble up the jungle above, eventually gaining the rib on the left and fresh air.

Irish Mail 66 metres   Very Difficult   (31.12.53)
On the right of the crag proper is a gully. The route starts in a little subsidiary gully on the left.
1 12m. Climb the gully; then take a high step up to the right.
2 27m. Move back to the obvious rake to the left, which leads to the shoulder left of the gully.
3 27m. *Quest for Corbeau* pitch 3.

Loosenard 60 metres   Severe   (22.3.52)
This is the ridge between the two branches of the gully. On suspect rock all the way. Climb steep and loose rock in two pitches of outstanding mediocrity, and vow never to return.

Winter Climbs

The winter routes all lie further to the right. The first takes the deep gully bounding the summer crag on its right.

The Cleaver 100 metres   *Winter* III
The gully is climbed in two main steps to a bay where there are two obvious exits. The right-hand branch is better.

The Final Cut 50 metres   *Winter* II/III
A pleasant though not outstanding route up the gully at the right-hand end of the lower cliff. It may be used as an introduction to the next route.

The following routes lie on the upper right cliff. This is almost pure heather in summer. In winter, several watercourses freeze and provide obvious lines. Belays may be hard to find.

★Rake End Wall 140 metres Winter III
At the start of the rake that divides the two sections of cliff a concave smear of ice lies on a rock slab. Climb the smear, moving left as it steepens to gain the obvious watercourse. Move right to the next groove and continue with some interest to the top.

Central Ice Falls 140 metres Winter III
Take the most appealing line up the obvious large area of ice to the right before the angle eases and the climbing degenerates into little more than scrambling through heather.

★Ice Mamba 140 metres Winter III
The obvious slim line of ice in the centre of the buttress. This is followed for two pitches to a small bay. Above is an ice pillar, which is avoided to the left at the given grade or may be climbed at grade V.

Heart of Ice 140 metres Winter III
Fifty metres to the right is a line leading to a prominent icicle fringe high on the crag. Easy ice leads to a steep icefall, at the top of which is the fringe. Avoid this by a deep gully on the left, or attempt:
Variation
Mr Drainpipe of Stockport 50 metres Winter V
The icicle fringe direct.

Nant Colwyn

Castell Castle   OS Ref 563 496
A delightful series of slabby buttresses on the south side of the ridge running down from Moel Lefn is known as Castell. The crags face north and east in a commanding position overlooking the Llyn Llewelyn and Beddgelert forest, with fine views beyond of Yr Wyddfa and the Nantlle Ridge, and they are easily seen from the footpath leading to Craig Cwm Trwsgl from Beddgelert forest. Despite the northerly aspect, the rock is clean and quick drying, and sheltered from the prevailing south-westerly winds.

Park at the Forestry Commission car-park near Pont Cae'r-gors between Beddgelert and Rhyd Ddu (OS Ref 575 502) and follow the footpath past Hafod Ruffydd Ganol and out of the forest to where the crags are clearly visible up to the left.

Alternatively, take the forestry tracks to Llyn Llewelyn and the track on the south side of the llyn until a small path leads steeply up through the forest on

NANT COLWYN and CWM PENNANT

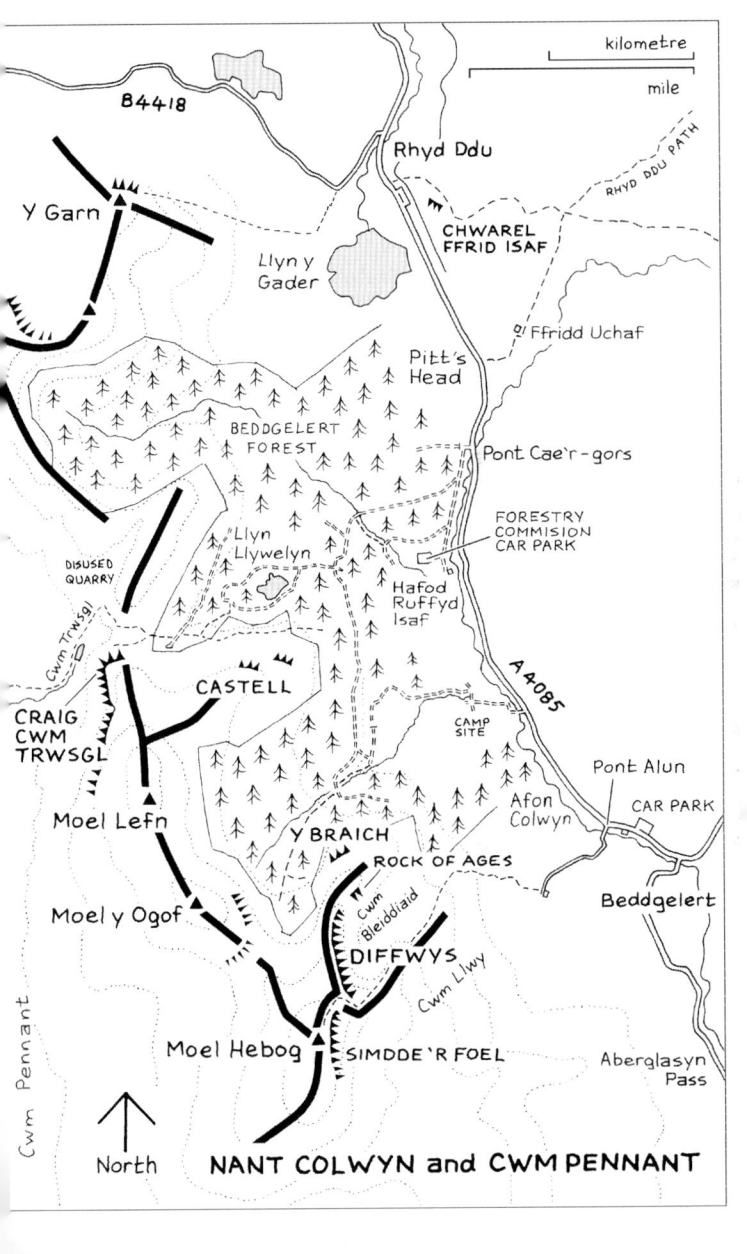

the left. Follow this to the edge of the forest and the crags are up the hill in front of you. Approach time: about 35 minutes.

The routes are all slabby, on clean rock, and about 15 to 20 metres high. They are located on three distinct sets of buttresses, and on each they are described **from right to left**.

Buttress One
This is located to the far west and slightly higher than the other buttresses, facing an easterly direction.

★**Titanium Rib** 20 metres   Severe 4a (10.9.01)
Climb the blunt rib on the right-hand side of the buttress

★**Tea with the Taliban** 20 metres   Very Severe 4c (17.9.01)
The depression in the centre of the buttress.

The Spies Came out of the Water
20 metres   Hard Very Severe 5a (10.9.01)
Climb straight up, 3 metres left of the preceding route.

Further to the left are some smaller problems up little walls and cracks.

Buttress Two
This is located about 60 metres lower down the ridge and faces the llyn. The routes are on the main buttress, which is some 18 metres high and has a rowan tree growing from the right-hand side of the crag. There is another, smaller, undercut buttress up and right, which also provides some sport.

Arabian Flights 20 metres   Very Severe 4c (17.9.01)
Climb up to the tree and so to the top.

★**Whose Skyline Is It Anyway** 20 metres   Very Severe 4c (17.9.01)
Climb the short corner and wall to reach the hanging groove to the left of *Arabian Flights*.

The Full Trash Can 20 metres   Very Severe 4c (17.9.01)
The corner left again.

Scarab Hunting 18 metres   Hard Very Severe 4c (17.9.01)
The almost protectionless blunt rib to the left.

Get a Sandal on This 18 metres   Very Severe 4c (17.9.01)
A short but sweet little slab up and left. Unprotected.

Buttress Three
Buttress Three is located lower down the ridge, just above the forest. It is about 15 metres high and consists of slabby compact rock. In the centre of the buttress is a large slab topped by a small wall.

Doctor Butt Says It's Easy Very Severe 5a (17.9.01)
Start at the right-hand side of the slab and climb diagonally to the top via the short wall above.

The Brown Runnel Very Severe 5a (17.9.01)
Follow the runnel diagonally rightwards to the top.

Mr Whippy Hard Severe 4b (17.9.01)
To the left is another slab with a lovely rippled hanging slab above. Climb it without any gear.

Running out of Rock Very Severe 4b (17.9.01)
The slab to the left.

Moel Hebog Bird Mountain

The fine peak and viewpoint of Moel Hebog is littered with crags of all shapes and sizes, the vast majority of which have long been neglected by climbers of all abilities despite the mountain's being able to claim the oldest recorded route in Wales. Unfortunately, much of the rock is very vegetated and somewhat damp, and all of the cliffs are slow to dry because of their aspect and elevation. When the cliffs *are* dry enough to be pleasant, most climbers will have their sights set on more interesting places, but they will be missing the solitude and magnificence of the Moel Hebog experience.

The climbing that exists is on two cliffs which both face east, and a third crag and its satellite which face north. The most southerly, Summit Cliff, overlooks Cwm Cŷd, and the main cliff, Y Diffwys, encircles the head of Cwm Bleiddiaid. Y Braich is found on the north side of the ridge of the same name that runs down from the summit area.

This area is botanically important. Before exploring here please refer to the note on page 14.

The easiest approach to Y Diffwys and the summit cliffs is via the normal walker's path from Beddgelert. This leaves the Beddgelert to Rhyd Ddu road about half a mile north of the village near to Y Warws and follows a private road to Cwm Cloch Farm by crossing the river at Pont Alun. The well-marked path runs right from here onto the hillside and then follows the grassy spur running up to the summit between Cwm Llwy and Cwm Bleiddiaid (not quite following the line of the right-of-way shown on the OS map). The cliffs of Y Diffwys are obvious in the back of the cwm on the right as one approaches the upper section of the path. The Summit Cliffs lie much further up on the left of the path.

The Summit Cliffs
OS Ref 567 467

These rather broken crags, overlooking Cwm Cŷd, bound the eastern side of the summit plateau for about three-quarters of a mile. The cliffs are split in the centre by a large gully, *Glyndŵr's Ladder* (otherwise known as Simdde'r Foel). Only a few routes exist but there is plenty of scope for more if you are that way inclined.

The buttress on the left of the gully, South Buttress, provides the following route:

Pursuer's Folly   72 metres   Very Difficult   (3.7.52)
Start at the lowest point of the buttress, immediately to the left of the bottom of the gully.
1 21m. Climb directly up the front of the buttress to the base of a double groove. Step round the sharp dividing nose to the right, and continue up the trough above for 6 metres. Move back left; then go right again at the top to the grassy terrace. Good block belay.
2 9m. Walk to the foot of the main wall and climb a depression on the right for 5 metres to reach a ledge 6 metres out from the gully.
3 18m. Climb the slab from the left-hand end of the ledge for 2 metres; then traverse to the left edge. Continue up this, over a block, to belay above.
4 24m. Scramble diagonally leftwards across the best of the available material, and gain the left edge above a vertical arête. Go along the narrow ridge to the summit plateau.

Glyndŵr's Ladder   75 metres   Easy   (c.1400)
A solo test-piece of its time! The gully offers a few short pitches interspersed with noisy scree and good rock scenery.

On the right of the gully is Ladder Buttress. The lower tiers of the buttress alongside the gully have been climbed at Very Difficult standard, but there are only two continuous routes here:

Wish I Could Be Elsewhere   45 metres   Very Severe   (25.9.01)
To the right of the gully is a hanging corner on the edge of Ladder Buttress.
1 27m. 4b. Climb direct through the corner and up to the ledge.
2 18m. Plod up to the top and walk off.

May Rib   46 metres   Difficult   (2.5.54)
To the right of Ladder Buttress is an isolated rib, formed by a series of short walls and topped by a longer one. Start at the bottom of the rib. Climb up three short walls to a stance at 12 metres. Ascend the obvious crack in the centre of the wall above, move round left into a corner, and then go back to the rib (18 metres). Follow a narrow, quartz-streaked ridge to the final wall, which is taken on the left to easy rocks and the top.

Y Diffwys   The Precipice   OS Ref 567 476

This, the main cliff of Moel Hebog, is some 120 metres high, although much is vegetated and easy-angled. It is split into two sections by a steep rake, The Companionway, which runs from left to right up the centre of the cliff. The South Cliff lies to the left and above the rake and the North Cliff below it on the right. The Companionway offers the quickest descent for climbs on the left-hand side of the North Cliff.

South Cliff

This is the large, broken, and vegetated cliff above the rake. It is concave and has a complex rib and groove structure. The routes are long and indefinite and defy detailed description (even by the first ascensionists).

Omega (105 metres Difficult) takes a vague line up the slabby left-hand side of the buttress, half-way between the walker's path and **Bending Groove** (135 metres Very Difficult 9.7.38), which climbs the central depression. A very heathery route, **Anaconda** (115 metres Very Difficult 15.4.53), takes a line diagonally right from the foot of Bending Groove. Two other routes, **Caterpillar** (115 metres Very Difficult 9.6.50) and **Lodestone** (90 metres Difficult 15.7.50), follow even fainter lines further to the right. This is an area for a true explorer.

The Companionway is the obvious easy rake, which begins at an easy chimney facing south and runs up diagonally rightwards between the two cliffs. In descent, keep well to the right (facing out) to avoid the upper reaches of Tension Crack on the North Cliff.

North Cliff

The North Cliff, below and to the right of The Companionway, is about 120 metres high. To the right of The Companionway the first obvious feature is a steep narrow gully, which is taken by Tension Crack. To the right again, before a less obvious break, is a compact area of rock with two pleasant routes. The cliff to the right is dominated in its lower half by large overhangs above wet slabs and grooves. These overhangs fade out to the right leaving a more heathery area before a huge patch of heather at about 15 metres, The Maidan, from which rises Maidan Gully. On the right of the gully is the easier-angled Maidan Buttress.

Tension Crack   80 metres   Severe   (3.8.50)
A good wet struggle. Start at a depression below an overhanging crack, with a cave above, some 18 metres right of the initial chimney of The Companionway.
1 14m. Climb a short wall to reach the overhanging crack. Follow this leftwards to a grassy recess and then continue more easily for 8 metres into the cave.
2 27m. Chimney up out of the cave on the left; then climb a strenuous wall beside the crack and step left to a narrow ledge. Continue straight up

the grassy bed of the main groove to a stance where it narrows and steepens again.
3 21m. Continue up the crack for 3 metres to a small chockstone, make a rising traverse across the left wall, and go delicately back into the crack above the impasse. Belay on the right.
4 18m. Scramble up to reach The Companionway.

Compression   130 metres   Very Severe   (9.56)
An interesting climb when in good condition. Start a few metres right of *Tension Crack* at an inconspicuous rib.
1 18m. Climb the rib on small holds to a small stance.
2 37m. Traverse slightly right to a crack beneath the overhang. Climb slabs for 6 metres to a thin crack, and go up to a second overhang. Climb over this at its right-hand end, and belay in a sort of gully to the right.
3 75m. Continue easily in several pitches up dirty slabs to the ridge.

Ignition   102 metres   Very Severe   (8.5.70)
A pleasant route, making the most of the buttress right of *Tension Crack*. Start on a rush-covered ledge beneath the obvious break to the right of *Tension Crack*.
1 18m. Climb the rib on the left and then a groove to gain a leftward-sloping gangway. Follow this to a wet crack, which is taken to a large grassy ledge. Large belay on the left.
2 24m. Move onto the slab above the belay and cross it to another grassy ledge on the left. Continue up the grass to a groove between two ribs. Follow the steep crack in the left wall until the rib can be reached and climbed to the overhang at the top. Step left across a groove and go up the obvious corner-crack to a grassy ledge on the skyline.
3 30m. Climb straight up for 6 metres; then traverse the pleasant slab on the right until the right edge of the overhang can be gained. Move back left on top of the overhang and continue up over easy ledges to a large block belay.
4 30 m. More easy climbing over heathery ledges gains The Companionway.

★**Redog**   58 metres   Hard Very Severe   (21.5.71)
A good climb on excellent rock towards the right of the central section, taking the left edge of the reddish slab capped by a huge overhang about 30 metres left of The Maidan. The foot of the slab is gained from the right. Start at a bulge, about 10 metres left of *Chinaman* and 6 metres right of two steep shallow grooves which run straight up to the bottom right-hand corner of the slab.
1 24m. Surmount the bulge, climb straight up for 5 metres, and then make a rising traverse left into the upper part of the right-hand groove. Climb this or the left rib to grassy ledges. Move left and go up to the highest ledge in the left-hand groove. Good stance and nut belay.
2 34m. 5a. Traverse out to a grassy ledge on the left edge of the slab. Go up near the edge, move right over a bulge, and step back left to continue near the arête to a ledge at 18 metres. Enter the groove above

Y Diffwys

- C The Companionway   S
- T Tension Crack   HVS
- R Redog
- M Maidan Gully   S

Moel Hebog Summit

Walkers' Path

SOUTH CLIFF

NORTH CLIFF

to ROCK OF AGES and Y BRAICH

MAIDAN BUTTRESS

THE MAIDAN

Craig CwmTrwsgl

1	The Arrow	E2
2	Efnisien	E1
3	The Exterminating Angel	E3
4	The Seraphic Sanction	E2
5	The Killing Fields	E4
6	Indefinite Article	E2
7	Day of Reckoning	E3
8	Blinded by the Light	E4
9	The Widening Gyre	E1

and climb it to a small triangular overhang. Step right to a crack and climb this and the wall above to grassy ledges. Nut belay.
The usual mixed grass and rock leads to the top.

Flashback 61 metres Hard Very Severe (23.8.84)
A more direct version of *Redog*.
1 24m. *Redog* pitch 1.
2 37m. 5a. Continue up the groove towards the overhang and move left to a poor resting-place. Traverse delicately left across the slab, step down, and move left to the arête. Climb the arête, and step right, then back left to a good nut belay.
Scramble to the top.

Chinaman 126 metres Very Difficult (9.6.50)
A poor, vegetated climb, based around the rightward-slanting chimney/groove-line to the left of The Maidan. Start at the foot of the chimney, about 10 metres left of the depression below the left-hand side of The Maidan.
1 37m. Climb the chimney for 6 metres; then traverse left to heather ledges, which are followed up leftwards to the foot of a wide groove. Move right out of this immediately and follow more heather rightwards to regain the original groove. Small spike belay on the right rib.
2 24m. Go up the bed of the groove into a dark little hole (The Opium Den). Climb out of this on the right and continue up the rib to the foot of a terrace. Move up left for 3 metres on a break which leads onto the front of the buttress.
3 65m. Continue leftwards along the break; then follow easy rocks in a direct line to the top.

Maidan Gully 130 metres Severe (9.6.51)
The obvious big gully above The Maidan gives one good steep pitch before it deteriorates. The route then follows *Maidan Buttress* to the top. Start on a grassy ledge above some easy rocks 10 metres right of *Chinaman* and at a scoop running up to the left corner of The Maidan.
1 18m. Climb the thin crack in the bed of the scoop for 9 metres until a move right can be made to The Maidan. Scramble up to a small cave (The Shrine) with a thread belay on the right.
2 21m. Walk up The Maidan to the gully.
3 24m. Climb awkwardly into the crack above and follow it into the bed of the gully. Scramble up to belay below a short step in the gully.
4 15m. Go up for 3 metres; then follow a ledge to the right and climb up rightwards to a stance on *Maidan Buttress*.
5 52m. *Maidan Buttress* pitch 6.

★Maidan Buttress 135 metres Difficult (18.5.51)
A good route up the buttress to the right of *Maidan Gully*. On the right of the buttress, starting 15 metres up, is a long and narrow pink or red slab. At the foot of the cliff and 15 metres to the right is a chimney.
1 15m. Climb the chimney or the rib on its right to a stance.

2 15m. Walk left to the foot of the pink slab.
3 18m. Follow an exposed ledge round the rib to the left to a ledge on the edge of the main buttress. Climb straight up the wall above to a small terrace below a dyke.
4 23m. From the right-hand end of the terrace, climb up to a niche. Step left and gain a second niche above. Climb the wall to the left, overlooking The Maidan, until the angle eases and a stance is reached.
5 12m. Continue up the edge to another stance.
6 52m. Climb the crest of the buttress, on perfect rock, to the top.

Pink Slab   120 metres   Severe   (13.7.50)
The obvious reddish, usually wet wet slab towards the right-hand side of the North Cliff. Reach its foot by the first two pitches of *Maidan Buttress*. Then climb the slab direct on small holds and go up to a stance and thread belay on top of a hanging pulpit. Step left and continue up the slab until two grooves lead into a scoop. Move up left and climb a short steep wall on good holds to gain the trough above. Continue up for 20 metres to a clean rib, which leads to the top.

Two Chimney Route   90 metres   Very Difficult   (6.1.50)
Start as for *Maidan Buttress*. Ascend the first chimney of *Maidan Buttress*; then continue up the more strenuous 25-metre chimney above. Scramble up to a terrace and follow it leftwards to finish up the pleasant rib at the top of *Pink Slab*.

To the right of the start of *Maidan Buttress* is a small buttress of good rock split by three steep fissures: **Toy Crack Climb** (Difficult 15.4.53) takes the right-hand of these and gives pleasant chimneying.

Finally, for true heather specialists, there is a high-level traverse of the North Cliff. This starts up *Maidan Buttress* and finishes on The Companionway.

Explorers' Traverse   175 metres   Difficult   (3.7.50)
A horticultural ramble in a good position.
1 48m. *Maidan Buttress* pitches 1, 2, & 3.
2 30m. Continue leftwards and then go up a slab to a small grassy patch. Climb the second slab on the left to gain The Maidan, and move across to a stance near the gully.
3 14m. Walk across for 5 metres; then climb up a slabby scoop, trending leftwards to reach the rib above The Opium Den of *Chinaman*. Climb the rib to a grassy stance.
4 9m. Wend up left to a stance on the edge.
5 15m. Continue traversing, ascending slightly, to a prominent spike. Climb over it, and move across the top of a steep chimney to reach a fine block belay 3 metres beyond.
6 18m. Ramble on easily on the same course to arrive at the right-bounding rib of the upper gully of *Compression*. Climb the rib up to a ledge leading into the gully, and go along to a stance below a short groove.

7 11m. Climb the groove to a stance.
8 30m. Continue up easily to emerge a few metres from the top of The Companionway.

It is possible to escape upwards at many points when you have had a surfeit of vegetation. If you do do the whole route, don't tell anyone for fear of ridicule!

The Rock of Ages

At a slightly lower level than Y Diffwys on the northern slope of Cwm Bleiddaid is an attractive little outcrop of excellent rock. It has many short pitches of about 12 metres that have all been climbed or reclimbed for the guide. A chimney cleaves the centre of the steepest part.

The chimney is Difficult. The hanging ramp to the left is **Terry's Rump** (E1 5b 25.9.01): gain the ramp, follow it leftwards, and exit right to finish; not desperate but devoid of the comfort of protection. Right of the chimney is **The Handcrack** (Very Severe 4c) as the name says. The wall right of the crack is **The Wall** (Very Severe 4c). The crack to the right runs to half height and is **The Fingercrack** (Hard Very Severe 5b).

Y Braich   The Arm   OS Ref 567 483

This crag lies on the north-western slopes of the ridge known as Y Braich, which runs down north-east from the summit of Moel Hebog. The crag faces north-north-west and lies at an altitude of 400 metres, making it an option only in still dry weather when the westerlies are not in full flow. The crag receives only the late afternoon sun, but then visitors will be rewarded with a fine vista of Coedwig Beddgelert and Yr Wyddfa.

Frm the Pont Cae'r-gors car-park (OS Ref 575 502), look towards Moel Hebog and walk up to the track on the right. Follow this to the left until a smaller path on the right can be taken after crossing the stream. At the next junction, turn left and follow the track, ignoring all left and right forks until the Afon Meillionen bridge is reached. A path leads up the right (true left) bank of the stream until you are clear of the forest. Contour left on the track outside the forest to its end. Y Braich can be clearly seen in front. Contour around to the base of the crag. (Approach time: 45 minutes.)

The climbing is predominantly slabby with the occasional overlap and crack.

The routes are described **from right to left**.

Deaf School   23 metres   Severe   (12.3.02)
Start up the right-hand side of the quartz block, below two grooves; then take the right-hand groove. Continue up the rightward-trending rib to finish up the cracked wall.

Buzzard Groove   23 metres   Very Difficult   (12.3.02)
Climb the right edge of the quartz block and follow the rib. Cross a heathery bay and climb the broken edge of the black mossy wall above.

★**Natty Dread** 23 metres   Severe 4a   (8.00)
Start at the left side of the block and go left to reach the groove. Climb steeply up this and move left onto a small pedestal. Move back right and follow the deep crack to the top.

Birth of Gravity 23 metres   Hard Very Severe 5a   (18.6.02)
Climb the obvious crack on the left, with the difficulties at the start.

No More Gain 23 metres   Hard Very Severe 5a   (21.9.02)
Climb the wall just left of the crack of *Birth of Gravity* past a couple pockets. A bit of an eliminate.

★**Not Taylor Made** 23 metres   E2 5c   (21.9.02)
The red bay to the left of the crack has an overlap at half height. Climb up to this, arrange some gear, which is somewhat unconvincing, and pull through the overlap on crimps. Finish more easily.

Wild Wind 23 metres   Severe   (18.6.02)
Take the stepped quartz wall to the left of the red bay until a ledge is reached. Go left before finishing directly.

Talaq Talaq Talaq 14 metres   E1 5b   (7.9.02)
Further left is a fine-looking blunt rib. Follow incipient cracks to an overlap in the wall right of the rib with micro-wires for protection.

★**Tropical Rain Rib** 14 metres   Very Severe 4b   (7.9.02)
Climb the rib.

Dark Summer 23 metres   Hard Very Severe 5a   (18.6.02)
Further left is a detached pinnacle. Climb its front face and the crack above until it is possible to pull left into a slight recess and finish direct.

★**Song for A Taylor** 21 metres   Severe 4a   (18.6.02)
Left of the pinnacle is a ramp-line. Follow this and continue in the diagonal until a V-groove is reached. Exit left and finish easily.

★**Spectrum** 21 metres   Severe 4a   (8.00)
At the extreme left of the crag is a slab that can be climbed anywhere at Very Difficult. On the right-hand side, climb the slab through an overlap. Continue up the broad rib, trending slightly right.

For those looking for some unusual entertainment, the white slab can be climbed, using the old metal fence-posts as fixed gear to give a V Diff sport route!

Y Braich Bach

Two hundred metres down the hillside and just above the trees is a black, north-facing, slabby dome, which provides a number of interesting routes on rock that tends to lack the reassurance of protection. The routes are 12 to 15 metres in length and described **from right to left**.

No More Flaying Very Severe 4c (21.9.02)
Start just left of the right-hand edge of the slab below a rightward-trending flake. Climb this to the top.

No More Slaying Very Severe 5a (21.9.02)
Start below a hanging flake just left and climb it to the top.

Ni Ydy'r Indians E1 5b (21.9.02)
Start right of the tree at the lowest part of the slab and climb up, trending slightly left, then right.

Fair and Squaw Very Severe 4c (21.9.02)
Start at the right-hand side of the upper slab and follow a slight corner.

Tomahawk Very Severe 4c (21.9.02)
Climb the slab to the left.

Ar y Drwm Hard Very Severe 5b (21.9.02)
Start below the bulge in the centre of the upper wall and climb through to the top.

No More Playing Very Severe 4c (21.9.02)
Climb the vague corner to the left.

More to Gain Very Severe 5a (21.9.02)
The final route follows the shattered wall at the extreme left before the crag merges with the forest.

Cwm Pennant

This beautiful valley contains one significant cliff, Craig Cwm Trwsgl, and a couple of pleasant outcrops. Rock and weather are generally similar to those of the Tremadog cliffs, although Craig Cwm Trwsgl, being higher and vegetated, is more prone to wet weather and much slower to dry.

In addition to the crags described, there are many isolated pitches scattered throughout the valley. These have gone unrecorded in the past and are left for readers to rediscover for themselves.

The cliffs are described as one approaches them up the valley. The first lies above Dolbenmaen Church.

Craig y Llan The Church Crag OS Ref 507 434
The short, isolated buttresses of this crag are very obvious from the Caernarfon to Porthmadog road. They can be approached through a gate on the left about 300 metres down the Cwm Pennant road from the church, and offer numerous possibilities for bouldering. Three climbs warrant

specific mention. About 300 metres along the track through the gate, and rather higher on the hillside, there is a prominent steep grey pillar of rock, with a fine crackline: **Buzzard Crack** (27 metres Very Severe). Just to its left is an obvious two-pitch buttress climb: **Grave Matters** (27 metres Hard Very Severe 5b c.1975). **Bombproof Runner** (E3 5c 11.5.88) is a mystery route 'to be found on the third outcrop away from the road'.

Craig Isallt   Lower Slopes Crag   OS Ref 533 450

A spur running down from Moel Hebog projects into Cwm Pennant and ends in a noticeable outcrop of rock. The main face of this lies to the south-west and is heavily vegetated. Climbing has been recorded here, and no doubt will be again, though it will never entertain anyone but the connoisseur of the esoteric. Two areas of rock are of more value. A series of slabby walls at the right-hand end of the crag gives some reasonable pitches in the Severe to Very Severe grades, some a little harder, reaching about 25 to 50 metres in height. Excellent bouldering may be enjoyed above the road on bulging outcrops of pillow-lava on the steep quarry face and also on slabby outcrops further along towards the main crag.

It is understood that the landowner **does not permit climbing** here. However, no problems are known to have been encountered in the past and, as it is possible that this situation will change anyway when CRoW is fully implemented, the decision has been taken to include these descriptions.

Craig Isallt is reached through a gate just beyond the bridge after Llanfihangel y Pennant.

South-West Face

The Ivy League   24 metres   Hard Very Severe 5a   (1997)
At the left-hand end of the main part of the crag is a rib with a stepped groove in it. Climb the groove with difficulty to exit onto the slab and trend rightwards to a tree belay. Abseil off.

To the right is a large area of grass and bracken, 'the field'.

The Schism   46 metres   Very Severe   (27.9.71)
The climb takes the obvious leftward-slanting dièdre left of the overhangs above pitch 1 of *Owl*. The second pitch is serious owing to lack of protection. Start at a slab beneath an overhang at the foot of the dièdre, reached by easy scrambling or by a short walk from the top of the rib of *Owl*.
1 9m. Traverse the slab rightwards to a good ledge. Break through the overhang with difficulty to gain small but good holds on the left. Continue to an ash tree.
2 37m. Climb directly behind the belay, past a gnarled stump and up the dièdre to an awkward thread runner. Move left and up, then back right to gain a slab. Pass a tiny grove of saplings, trend left to a niche, and swing onto a slab (hidden foothold down left). Climb the thin slab to a hard pull

onto poor holds. Break left and climb a rib bounding a black slab on its left. Small spike belay on the edge of the slab.

Owl 82 metres Severe (26.6.54)
The large field is reached by the prominent rib below its left-hand end, after which the overhanging upper wall is taken on the right. Start at the base of the rib, which is split by a crack.
1 34m. Climb the rib to belays on the edge of the field.
2 18m. Go up and slightly right to a tree under a line of overhangs. Climb up rightwards and awkwardly move round onto the face of the buttress. Traverse right to the belays below the groove on the right.
3 30m. Climb the groove, keeping to the right at first, until an exit can be made to a shelf on the left. Traverse left and go up easily to a belay. Scrambling remains.

The buttress to the right of *Owl* is heavily vegetated. Further right is:

South-East Wing
The first feature of the wing is the steep Ivy Buttress (above a fence) that forms the right-hand edge of the South-West Face. Two routes have been recorded hereabouts but no descriptions have been forthcoming: **Left-Hand Route** (2.4.56) on the left-hand side of Ivy Buttress, and **Left-Hand Route Direct** (HVS A2 2.6.56), which takes a thin crack on pegs.

Sundance 50 metres Severe (27.9.71)
A pleasant and varied line, the most continuous on the face. Escape below the crux is unfortunately possible. Start under the pedestal at the foot of the clean slab just left of Ivy Buttress.
1 8m. Gain the top of the pedestal, preferably by its left edge. Belay by the V-chimney.
2 24m. Climb the V-chimney and the interesting crack above. From the good ledge at 9 metres, step right to a niche. Soon a high step right leads to easier-angled slabs. Continue to a large perched block.
3 18m. Take a direct line to the top left-hand corner of the slab and step round to an insecure turf ledge. Delightful climbing now leads via little slabby overhangs directly to the top.

Slab Route 27 metres Hard Very Severe (24.12.55)
The steep slab in the bay immediately left of Ivy Buttress has been climbed. (The 1955 route may have taken an easier line. The HVS line was recorded in 2.91.)

Yonec 45 metres Severe (22.6.71)
The obvious line of chimneys on the left flank of the buttress, pleasant and not too serious. Start in the corner 5 metres left of the fence.
1 14m. Climb the corner-chimneys until a traverse right leads to a little flake pinnacle directly above the fence. Step up left into the continuation chimney and climb the through-route from the depths of the lower chimney to the top of the upper chimney.

2 17m. A short crack leads to another chimney, steep and narrow at first, which eases to give access to the top of a large pinnacle. Step across the top of the chimney to belay on a ledge on the buttress.
3 6m. An easy curving chimney, or the rib on its left, leads to a miniature col. Belay on the right.
4 8m. Traverse 5 metres right to a hidden chimney, narrow and awkward, and climb it.
Either scramble to the top or follow the final 11 metres of *Ivy Buttress*.

Menna   61 metres   Very Severe   (24.2.83)
Start immediately right of the fence.
1 15m. 4c. Climb the thin crack in the front of the rib, surmounting a small bulge half-way.
2 23m. Climb the wide chimney and continue easily up the rib until able to traverse left across vegetation to a large tree underneath the steeper part of the crag.
3 23m. 4c. Climb the crack to the overhang and move out left to reach excellent holds. Step up left with difficulty and then hand-traverse out right to the arête. Finish up easy slabs.

Ivy Buttress   54 metres   Severe   (26.6.54)
A pleasant route, which takes the buttress direct. Start below an obvious break about 6 metres right of the fence.
1 18m. Climb a small crack to a ledge on the right-hand edge of the buttress; then go straight up the corner to a good ledge.
2 18m. Climb the slab above the ledge to a large tree; then follow the arête to a large oak tree and good belays.
3 18m. Ascend the easy-angled rib to the overhang. Surmount this on the right and continue up the slab to finish.
Variation
Start just right of the fence and climb the steep crack, then the headwall of the ordinary finish.

Easter Wall   37 metres   Hard Very Severe 4c   (2.4.56)
One of the better routes here, steep and delicate, but with some dubious holds. Start about 12 metres right of *Ivy Buttress*, below a clean orange-coloured wall. Climb up to a small tree; then go straight up a faint weakness in the wall above to a scoop and a large grassy ledge and spike belay. Finish up pitch 3 of *Ivy Buttress*.

To the right the crag becomes more featured. The first main feature is a prominent forested recess: **The Cracks** (30 metres Very Difficult 1956). Right again is an obvious chimney capped by a chockstone: **The Chasm** (30 metres Severe 10.8.56).

Sweeper   24 metres   Very Severe 4b/c   (10.7.95)
The wall left of *Swept Wall*. Hardly worth the effort.

Swept Wall   30 metres   Severe   (10.8.56)
A fine steep pitch at an amenable grade. Start at a shallow groove in the centre of the right-hand wall of *The Chasm*. Climb the groove and the wall above to two large and loose spikes. Make a rising traverse rightwards and then go diagonally leftwards to the top of the wall. The short wall at the back of the bay leads to the top.

Schwept   24 metres   Severe   (20.5.95)
The clean arête and wall just right of *Swept Wall*.

Spreadeagle   30 metres   Very Severe   (22.6.71)
Another poor climb, taking the corner and slab between *Swept Wall* and *Oak Tree Wall*.

Oak Tree Wall   30 metres   Very Severe   (3.6.56)
A good delicate pitch on the next slab to the right of *Swept Wall*. Start on a pointed block. Step left from the block onto the slab and move across into a shallow groove. Ascend this to a large oak tree on the left, traverse right, and climb the delicate slab, bearing right.

The cliff now rapidly deteriorates, becoming much shorter and covered in ivy.

Craig Cwm Trwsgl   Rough Hollow Crag   OS Ref 550 494

This rambling cliff at the head of Cwm Pennant lies on a northerly shoulder of Moel Lefn. The rock is a superb, rough dolerite redolent of the best of Tremadog; and much of the cliff has a pleasant westerly aspect, though the left-hand and better end faces north-west. Much of the cliff is broken, but it is very large and there are substantial areas of rock amongst the vegetation.

The crag is best approached either by driving to the head of Cwm Pennant and following the Bwlch y Ddwy-elor track to the reservoir beneath the cliff, or (a shorter drive for those based to the north, and an easier walk) by driving into Beddgelert Forest at Pont Cae'r-gors, between Beddgelert and Rhyd Ddu, parking near Hafod Ruffyd (OS Ref 575 502), and taking the Bwlch Cwm Trwsgl path along forestry tracks and paths from there. This takes around 40 minutes.

The cliff is best viewed from the old winding-house on the opposite side of the lake, which is the only point from where all the areas can be easily identified. It extends for around half a mile in all and divides into three main climbing sections. From left to right:

First, well round to the north, and not visible from lower on the Cwm Pennant approach, there is a fine diamond-shaped slab, the jewel of Cwm Pennant. This is the location of *The Exterminating Angel* and the subsequent modern routes. There is another similar buttress to its right, just before the next section.

As the crag begins to turn, a drystone wall runs up to the foot of the cliff. To the left of this there is a mass of rock in the upper half of the crag characterized by a rib-and-groove structure with massive overhangs. *The Widening Gyre* and *Mere Anarchy* are to be found here.

The central section of the cliff reveals two long ribs bounding a heathery recess and running up to a large overhang with a clean area of rock above. The ribs are taken by *Helix* and *The Second Coming*. Right again, a steep red tower just before a heathery gully is climbed by *The Ceremony of Innocence*.

Much further over to the right, across several hundred metres of broken ground and at a higher level, is another short but very steep outcrop on which one or two difficult routes have been made, notably the prominent groove in the right wall of a deep gully. This is E3 5c, and much shorter than it appears.

Those used to well-developed crags with a network of climbs should note that with only a handful of routes in over 800 metres of crag, the routes here are well separated, especially since eight of the routes are on the one compact buttress. However, much of the intervening ground has been left for a reason – copious amounts of vegetation.

The easiest descent from all routes is well over to the left of the cliff.

See page 96b for diagram.

Tu Tin Tut   100 metres   Severe   (9.5.54)
The route climbs the rib rising from the wall at the north-west corner of the cliff. Take stances at will. Start above the wall below the rib. The slabby rib with occasional stances is followed to a grassy terrace below an overhanging wall. Traverse right across slabs below overhangs for 6 metres. Climb a corner; then move right to a recess, from which the foot of a large slab to the right can be gained. Climb the slab and take the top overhang on the left. Finish easily up slabs.

To the right is the best part of the cliff, the aforementioned diamond-shaped slab. This is composed of near-perfect dolerite with excellent friction, though it often appears damper than is the case. The first four routes all finish at good nut belays on the ledge at the top of the striking crackline of *Efnisien*.

Somewhat incredibly, a route has been claimed on the slabby front face of the largest boulder beneath this part of the cliff. If you are that desperate, find your own way.

★★**The Arrow**   37 metres   E2 5c   (4.5.95)
This route takes a line just to the left of, and parallel to, the crackline of *Efnisien*, aiming for the prominent eponymously-shaped niche high on the left of the slab. Start at a short chimney at the left-hand side of the slab. Climb the chimney and step onto the wall on the right. Climb the slab via the cleaned line, aiming just to the right of the two patches of vegetation, until a bold move gains the niche. Finish as for *Efnisien*, round the left side of the final block.

★★**Efnisien**   37 metres   E1 5b   (9.74)
This is the striking diagonal crackline that runs the full height of the slab.
Start just right of the left-hand bottom corner of the slab beneath the
overhanging crack. The initial section to the horizontal break at 12 metres
proves trying. The slanting crack above, though easier, offers sustained
climbing to reach an awkward finish leftwards around the final block.

★★★**The Exterminating Angel**   42 metres   E3   (9.74)
The original gem of the diamond-shaped slab. Although low in the grade
it is definitely harder for the short. Start below a fluted tongue of rock,
directly beneath the ledge and tree in the middle of the slab.
1 18m. 5c. Climb the V-chimney on the right of the fluted tongue to a
foot-ledge on the left. Climb diagonally leftwards, aiming for a fragile
spike beneath the right-hand end of the overlap. Step left and climb the
overlap; then trend rightwards across the slab to reach the ledge.
2 24m. 5b. Climb onto a flake above the belay niche. Move left onto the
wall to gain a slanting shelf. Climb the centre of the slab above, passing a
diamond-shaped niche, until a delicate pull into a shallow scoop is made.
Step right and follow the seam to the ledge. A surprising pitch.

★★**The Seraphic Sanction**   49 metres   E2   (31.7.87)
The vague groove/scoop to the right of *The Exterminating Angel* provides
an enjoyable climb.
1 35m. 5b. Follow *The Exterminating Angel* for 5 metres; then trend
rightwards and climb a vague groove to a short impending wall. Pull over
on the left, and move right to a cracked wall. Climb the wall, bearing
slightly right to join an easy crack, which leads leftwards to a block belay.
2 14m. 5a. Climb the innocuous-looking scoop behind to easy ground
and the ledge.

The Killing Fields   55 metres   E4   (31.7.87)
The right arête of the slab is starkly under-protected. Start at the foot of a
dirty groove, just right of the rib.
1 21m. 5c. A few metres of wet rock lead up the slab left of the rib.
Climb this to a thin horizontal break and some protection – the last!
Continue up the slab above, passing a difficult overlap, and finish with a
worrying mantelshelf onto a rounded ledge.
2 34m. 5b. Step round rightwards to enter a fine overhanging crack,
which is followed until the rib is reached. Climb the rib to a ledge, and
finish up a higher rib above.

Indefinite Article   72 metres   E2   (1996)
To the right, past a grotty gully, is a shallow rib. This provides the substance
of the route, which is rather dirty at present.
1 23m. 5b. Climb directly up the left-hand side of the rib to a
poorly-protected crux, and traverse right at the top to belay beneath an
overhanging crack.
2 49m. 5a. Climb the leftward-slanting crack; then continue up the rib
above to the pegs at the top of *The Exterminating Angel*.

Thirty metres right again is a superb wall supported by a lower buttress, providing the substance of the next two routes.

Blinded by the Light 61 metres E4 (1992)
A similar line to *Day of Reckoning*.
1 21m. 5b. *Day of Reckoning* pitch 1.
2 40m. 6a. Scramble leftwards up the vegetated ledge for 8 metres; then aim up right along the crackline past a peg to the arête. Climb the crack in the arête, traverse left, and go to the top on jugs.

★★★**Day of Reckoning** 55 metres E3 (31.7.87)
A tremendous route with superb climbing in a fine position.
1 21m. 5b. Directly below the wall is an easy-looking rib of clean rock on the right. Climb the rib to a surprisingly difficult exit, and move leftwards up a grassy ramp to belay beneath the cracks.
2 34m. 5c. Climb the right-slanting crack until good holds lead back left to the centre of the wall. Climb the crack above to a tiny niche and move right with difficulty to gain a layaway edge. Move back left and up to enter a shallow groove, and go to the top.

The next section of rock lies above and to the right of *Day of Reckoning* and has a steep rib-and-groove structure. However, an area of steep heather must be negotiated before climbing can commence. Prominent features are an immense overhang at about half height on the left, and a short, bottomless chimney high on the right.

Mere Anarchy 45 metres Hard Very Severe (5.76)
Start at the foot of the rib which bounds the left-hand side of the slab beneath the obvious large overhang.
1 21m. 5a. Climb the rib until at its top a difficult move can be made up right into a groove above the overhang. Climb the groove for a couple of metres until a move back left can be made; then go up to a small stance and nut belays.
2 18m. 4a. The groove on the right leads to a ledge with loose blocks. Climb the wall behind to a heathery rake and go left to the foot of a crack.
3 6m. 4c. Climb the crack.

The Widening Gyre 76 metres E1 (5.75)
The route follows the central corner and crackline of this part of the cliff, making a direct line up the buttress at its highest point. Start by scrambling up steep heathery grooves to the right-hand corner of the slab beneath the huge overhang.
1 46m. 5b. Follow a heathery ramp up right until directly below the corner. Climb the mossy slab into this, and follow it to a small overhang. Layback to a large overhang and climb it with difficulty to good holds above. Climb the groove to a grassy bay, from which a short crack on the right leads to a higher bay. Belay left of the prominent chimney.
2 30m. 4a. Move round to a ledge on the left, and climb the crack up the slab above to finish.

The next routes are some 200 metres to the right of the stone wall, but they can be difficult to distinguish from many other similar features in the area just right of the wall. The main feature is a large, smooth, undercut wall high on the crag. The first two routes take the ribs that run up to each end of this wall.

Helix 108 metres E1   (22.8.66)
The route follows the left-hand rib and then grooves above through the top wall. An impressive top section, though the lower part is much easier and rather artificial. Start by scrambling up heather to a very short layback corner at the base of the left-hand rib.
1 12m. Climb the corner and a slab above; then move left at the top to a grass ledge and block belay.
2 21m. Climb a short wall to the left on good holds, then up a small slab. Step left onto a rib and traverse left into a corner, which is climbed to a large ledge with peg belays.
3 15m. Climb the corner-crack on the right until a hand-traverse allows a further move right. Go straight up to a ledge.
4 30m. 5b. Move round to the right and climb over a small overhang to enter an obvious groove. Climb the groove to a roof, move left, and go up to a slab. Climb this to a corner.
5 30m. Climb the groove left of the belay to the top.

The Second Coming 85 metres E1   (4.75)
Start just left of the base of the right-hand rib, right of a prominent overhang.
1 15m. Climb a groove on the left for a couple of metres, and then up right to gain the narrow crest of the rib. Follow this to its top, and traverse rightwards to a grassy bay and belays.
2 18m. Climb the short corner behind the belay to steep heather leading rightwards to a block belay beneath the overhanging corner.
3 37m. 5a. Climb strenuously up the corner into a niche. A groove leads right to a rib, which is climbed for a short distance until a traverse left can be made across a groove to a good flake. Follow the open groove to a grass ledge and spike belays on the left.
4 15m. 5c. Step back right and move up to a good spike. Cross the wall to the left with difficulty to gain a shallow groove, which leads to the top.

The Ceremony of Innocence 61 metres Very Severe   (1975)
This climb takes the steep red pillar to the right of the main cliff. Start below and right of the pillar, at a little rib standing out from the heather and reached by very steep heathery climbing.
1 34m. 5a. Climb the rib to a heathery landing, and traverse left into a scooped groove, which is taken to a ledge on the left. Move up the wall on good holds to gain a foot-ledge on the left with difficulty. Climb leftwards up the slab into its left-bounding groove, and up this to a poor stance and belay.
2 27m. 4b. Traverse into the centre of the slab and climb it, with disappointing ease, to gain a niche. Move left to finish up the slab and the steeper groove ahead.

In the past, several easier routes have been described on the more broken sections of this cliff, but they are now left for those who feel so inclined to disengage them from their native heather.

The quartz-speckled slabs high on Moel Lefn, which are clearly visible from Bwlch y Ddwy-elor, give pleasant, easy-angled pitches of around 20 metres, but are not really much use for anything other than a pleasant diversion whilst walking the ridge leading to Moel yr Ogof and Moel Hebog.

'On the East Arête of Y Garn'
Reproduced from *A Climber's Guide to Snowdon and the Beddgelert District* by H R C Carr (1926)
Eastern Arête (1905)   Climbers and photographer unknown

First Ascents

No first ascent details have been discovered for Saxifrage Rib, Raven Buttress, Dobbin; Tower Chimney; Ebon Ridge; The Handcrack, The Wall, The Finger-Crack; Buzzard Crack; The Cracks, The Chasm.

c.1400	**Glyndŵr's Ladder** O Glyndŵr	

On sight solo. A strong English party failed to follow!

1905   **Castell Cidwm Gully, Wolf's Buttress, Pinnacle Ridge, Eastern Arête**   W P Haskett Smith *et al.*

'Here [Castell Cidwm Gully] there are two capital bits which make one wish to have either four hands or four feet, as most of the excellent handholds are towards the same side of the gully and most of the equally fine footholds are just out of reach on the opposite side.' (W P H S, C C Journal 1905)

'It has three pitches. The first is a dark wet cave at 40 feet high, which is climbed to the right of the capstone, where one bush assists and another impedes the progress of the climber.' (1926 guide)

'This route can hardly be regarded as much of an achievement, for there is only 15 feet of climbing.' (New Climbs 1966)

'Passing through some fallen blocks at the very foot [of Eastern Arête] you are forced to the left, and find a square angle, and mounting on a sort of wardrobe on the right you work up in the angle. Personally I found it a place where, when the second man joined me on top of the wardrobe, my peace of mind was substantially increased.' (CC Journal 1905)

Obviously climbers had as much difficulty in describing their art then as today.

1910   **Sentries' Ridge**   J M A Thomson, H O Jones, K J P Orton

1911 Easter   **North Gully, Central Ridge**   H M F Dodd, J M A Thomson

'On the stiff upper passage the leader could certainly be aided, but on the lower this would hardly be possible.' (H R C Carr on North Gully)

1911 Easter   **The Grey Gully and Wall**   H O Jones, Miss B Jones, K J P Orton, Mrs Orton

Not by the line described, which was climbed by B K Barber and A S Pigott on 12.6.38.

'An easy scramble is succeeded by 70 feet of climbing similar to that in the Bracket Gully on Lliwedd.'

1911 Easter   **Five Cave Gully**   H O Jones, R Todhunter (AL) L Noon

'Todhunter and Noon boldly bid for a gargantuan mouth away on the left.' (CC Journal 1912)

'A second but steeper groove is then tackled, and a mantelshelf five feet higher attained. Both these grooves entail a strenuous struggle, whose severity the second man can only slightly mitigate with a push. The third man, meanwhile is wedged in the cave, but his opportunities for anchoring are hardly adequate.' (J M A Thomson)

1911 Easter   **Adam Rib**   J M A Thomson and party

A fine start to exploration on a new crag. They avoided the final

112 First Ascents

pitch by traversing into Eden Gully. The final pitch and the more direct line described were climbed by G H L Mallory and R Todhunter in 9.12.

1911 Easter   **Knight's Move Climb**   J M A Thomson and party
The present start was climbed by M W Guiness, G L Reid, and Miss Hughes on 30.5.25.

1911 Easter   **Grass Pitch Gully**   J M A Thomson and party
'Leader needs 30 feet of rope and anything likely to assist him in clinging to precipitous vegetation.'
The grass pitch disappeared in 1945 but it is not known who disappeared with it!

1911 Easter   **Lichen Ridge**   J M A Thomson and party
'Conscientious adherence to rock ensures an agreeable climb.'
Little is known about the initial exploration of Craig Cwm Du, but Thomson initially pioneered twelve routes which varied from Moderate to Exceedingly Difficult. One of them: 'A certain gully pitch has characteristics that are unique within the combined knowledge of our party.' Thompson's party did, however, return at Whitsuntide, staying at the Snowdon Ranger Hotel. It consisted of W A Brigg, W P Haskett Smith, Dr L Noon, Mrs Orton, Prof J P Orton, and of course Thomson. On the Friday evening they ascended a new route of interest at Castell Cidwm. On the Saturday they did a new gully on Mynydd Mawr which yielded a 'pretty climb with an airy face finish. The East Ridge of Y Garn, destined some day to become a favourite expedition, occupied Sunday. The last day was devoted to Llechog.'

1911 Whitsun   **The Mermaid Climb, Central Rib**   J M A Thomson, W P Haskett Smith, W A Brigg
'It will be gathered at once from the name [of the former] that this climb presents to the eye an attractive front, but tails off not far from the middle.' (Awful puns in route names are nothing new, it seems.) 'It will be gathered that steadiness and precision of movement will be necessary throughout the climb. The leader cannot be aided. The rock is of splendid quality, and, to the best of my recollection, not a single fragment was removed. To strong parties, and to them only, The Central Rib can be recommended without reserve.'

1911 June 18   **Black Rib, Torpedo Route, Cloister Climb**   J M A Thomson, H O Jones, Mrs Orton
[Black Rib]: 'A leaf on the right has to be seized at a given moment with a stretching reach, otherwise the problem is apt to prove puzzling and to cause ingeniously intricate poses of the body.' (CC Journal 1912)
'As Cloister Climb was our third ascent of the day, our party may possibly have slightly overrated its difficulty, but we were certainly impressed with the severity of some of the passages encountered.'

1911 Sept   **Eastern Gutter, Trinity Buttress B**   G H L Mallory, H E L Porter
Both of these routes were 'lost' for many years as a result of poor descriptions. There must be a moral here for all first ascensionists! Trinity Buttress was rediscovered in June 1938 by B K Barber, A S Pigott and F Solari. Eastern Gutter had to wait until 4.5.80 for its re-identification and the second ascent by H I Banner and

Central Variant (HVS), Craig yr Ogof
Climber: Pat Cocks   Photo: Martin Whitaker

The Devils (E3), Craig y Bera
(first ascent, 1998)
Climber: Pat Littlejohn
Photo: Littlejohn col.

M Yates. Is this the longest period between ascents for a British climb?

1911 Sept **Mallory's Ridge**   H E L Porter, G H L Mallory
A fine climb which was unjustifiably neglected since it had acquired a notorious reputation for difficulty and looseness leading to its omission from Carr's guide. The line described is that taken on the second ascent by E W Dance, W Gordon, G Eglington on 18.9.49. The two variations to the crux pitch were climbed by D Clutterbuck, P L B Pilling on 10.8.51 and H Storey, F Gandy on 15.7.56.

'In Cumberland the first question one is always asked about Wales is "But isn't the rock very loose?" There is much more rock in Wales.' (John Laycock, FRCC Journal 1912)

1911 Sept **Four-Pitch Gully**   G H L Mallory, R Todhunter
The start of climbing in Cwm Silyn, but why this?

1912 Sept **Pis-Aller Rib, Yellow Buttress**   G H L Mallory, R Todhunter

1913 **Sunset Rib**   R Todhunter, G L Keynes, R Muhlberg
The first route on the crag. It was to be another twelve years before it had a companion.

1913 **Trinity Buttress C**   R Todhunter, G L Keynes, H A H Percy, G H L Mallory
Another lost route which was finally located and re-ascended by B K Barber, A S Pigott, and J R Jenkins on 15.5.38.

1920 Whitsun **South Buttress, North Buttress**   E W Steeple, G Barlow, A H Doughty

1925 April 10 **Overhanging Chimneys**   E Downes, H R C Carr, W McNaught
Carr, having extensively explored Llechog, now turned his attentions and exploring talent to the Cwm Silyn crags.
'Calling loudly upon the patron saint of the locality, the leader explores the smooth vertical face with eager fingers. The saint, responsive to so urgent a request, opens a cunning little cavity in the rock precisely where it is least expected and most desired. The thankful climber is now able to swing out boldly across the wall and quickly gains the security of the chimney.'
After the inclusion of this route in an early selected climbs guide to Snowdonia, 'Ron Davies is a t**t' could be found inscribed at the top of the route.
Maurice's Crack was climbed on 25.8.25 by M W Guiness, M S Gotch, H R C Carr, W McMillan.
Terror Infirmer was climbed on 13.4.52 A J J Moulam, J H Longland, F L Mayo, J L Longland: '...and then enter the crack. The manœuvre is strongly reminiscent of the start of Kern Knotts Crack. The crack itself is just as steep as the Cumbrian rival but demands delicate balance rather than strenuous exertion.'

1925 April 10 **Engineers' Climb**   E Downes, G A Lister
1925 April 12 **Deep Chimney**   H R C Carr W McMillan, W McNaught
1925 April **The Recess Route**   E Downes, H R C Carr, E Hewitt, W McNaught, W McMillan
1925 April **Artist's Climb**   H R C Carr, D Hewitt
1925 April **Original Route**   M G Bradley, B F K O'Malley
1925 Aug 22 **Nirvana Wall**   H R C Carr, W K McMillan
'Hardly the height of attainment.' (1971 guide)

1925	**L.M.H.** Oxford University Women's Mountaineering Club party. *The party was from Lady Margaret Hall. So now you know.*
1926 April 4	**Ordinary Route** D R Pye, W R Reade, C A Elliot, N E Odell *First known as The Great Slab Route. The Inside Variation appears to have been climbed at the same time. The Inside Finish was climbed by J B Joyce on 8.9.35.*
1926	**A Climber's Guide to Snowdon and the Beddgelert District by Herbert R C Carr** *The very first Climbers' Club guidebook had been published in 1909: Climbs on Lliwedd edited by J M Archer Thomson and A W Andrews. Climbing in the Ogwen District, also by Thomson, followed a year later. Work started on a third volume covering the remainder of Snowdonia, for which Thomson was joined by G H L Mallory, who was later assisted by R Todhunter. However, the war and Everest intervened and it was left to the enthusiastic young Carr to complete the work. The book covers not only the rock climbs then known, but includes also full descriptions of walks, ridges, hills, and cwms.*
1927	**Direct Route** *No-one appears to have claimed this route though the lower part as described was climbed by Kirkus a few years after this date.*
1928 Aug 28	**The Scarf** E Downes, H R C Carr, E D Ritchie, B H Bathurst
1931 May 31	**Kirkus's Route** C F Kirkus, G G Macphee *They climbed separate finishes! – Macphee's being closer to that now described. This was first recorded by G C Band, E A Wrangham 13.4.52: see Central Variant. The route was originally known as Right-Hand Route.*
1931 Whitsun	**Non-Engineers Climb** R D Graham, G W Anson
1931 July 14	**Outside Edge Route** J M Edwards, C H S R Palmer *One of the great Welsh mountain classics. A fine find from Edwards. 'Foully wet. Some rain every day this fortnight; usually much rain.' (Menlove by Jim Perrin). Modern visitors often have the same problem. The direct start was added by D Clutterbuck, H L Kool on 2.7.51.*
1931 Aug 2	**Upper Slab Climb** C F Kirkus, A B Hargreaves, A W Bridge *On an early repeat, Hargreaves led in stockings and J M Edwards followed in hobnails. Care was taken on the stances!*
1933 March 26	**Bedrock Gully, Sweep Wall** J M Edwards *Probable first winter ascent of the gully: A Liddel, A G Cram 9.2.69.*
1933 Sept 6	**Black Gully** G G Cruikshank *The gully epoch seems to have reached Cwm Silyn somewhat later than the rest of the country. It is also somewhat amazing that it took until this time to explore the possibilities of the Cwm Silyn gullies.*
1935 April 19	**The Little Kitchen** J M Edwards *'The view is good and the rock not so good. There was also water in the place and mosses. Sandy (Edge) saw all this and remained where the little avalanches would not reach.'(J M Edwards)*
1936 July 22	**Rib and Tower** J E Q Barford, R B Kemball-Cook *The route described differs slightly from the original and coincides with Fay Cee Rib climbed by B Wright on 8.7.45.*

First Ascents 115

1938 July 9	**Bending Groove** H T Jackson, P Wareing, S Styles
1938 Aug 12	**Jezebel** B K Barber, A S Pigott, J E Byrom
1939 May	**Bankers' Buttress** J E Byrom, J Lomas
1946 July 5	**Angel Pavement** C P Brown, A J J Moulam (AL)

Direct finish: A J J Moulam, Miss V A Jones, 17.3.52.
Left-hand finish: P R Littlejohn, J Littlejohn, 8.4.97.
One of the better routes on Craig y Bera, certainly the only one to achieve any sort of popularity.

1946 Aug 4	**Oblique Route** C P Brown, J P Cooper

The main part to the cave had certainly been descended in 1935 by J P Cooper and party after reaching the Ogof, though by which route they reached it is uncertain.

1948 June 16	**Reunion Cracks** P R Hodgkinson, J Gianelli
1949 Feb 24	**Residents' Wall** P O Work, G W Staunton
1949 June 4	**Jericho** R G Folkard, P Wilkinson
1949 June 5	**Gardener's Gully** R G Folkard, P Wilkinson
1949 Sept 17	**Slab and Groove** E W Dance, W Gordon
1949 Sept 18	**Nadroedd** E W Dance, W Gordon
1949 Oct 16	**Primrose Path** P R Hodgkinson, J Gianelli
1949 Dec 29	**Eve's Folly** J T Hughes, K E Oldham
1950 Jan 6	**Two Chimney Route** P O Work, D E Dublin

'A good bad weather route.'

1950 April 9	**Lamb's Leap** D Sutton, W, Gordon
1950 April 9	**Manchester Rib** R B Clayton, M Fenton

Climbed in mistake for Pis-Aller Rib.

1950 May 12	**Leo's Wall, Fox Route, Oppenauer Slab** R B Clayton, G W Wood

The 1971 guidebook describes these routes as being recommended when the cliff is intolerably crowded.

1950 June 9	**Caterpillar, Chinaman** P O Work, B E Nicholson

The start of a perverse enthusiasm for this rather unfashionable cliff.

1950 June 22	**Omega** P O Work, G W Staunton
1950 June 25	**Finale Wall** N A Thomson, G Eglington

Also recorded as Finals Wall.

1950 July 3	**Explorers' Traverse** P O Work, T W Hughes
1950 July 13	**Pink Slab** P O Work, M Rowland, G W Staunton
1950 July 15	**Lodestone** B E Nicholson, G W Staunton
1950 July 25	**The Bar Steward** F G Dennis, R C Davies

Awful puns rear their head again.

1950 Aug 3	**Tension Crack** F Ashton, F, Gough, G W Staunton, P O Work
1951 May 18	**Maidan Buttress** J Derry, D Meigh
1951 June 7	**Colin's Gully** C B Wilson, E A Wrangham, J F Adams, A Wailes-Fairbairn
1951 June 9	**Maidan Gully** E W Dance, G Eglington, A E Davies

New gullies continued to appear.

1951 June 9	**The Greenhouse Roof** K B Oldham, P Wadsworth, G Eglington
1951	**Kirkus's Direct** V Ridgeway and party

Pitch 3 was added by B Ingle and R G Wilson on 20.5.63 thinking the entire route to be new.

1952 March 17	**No Highway** A J J Moulam, Miss V A Jones
1952 March 22	**Quest for Corbeau, Loosenard** A J J Moulam, J M Barr

1952 April 13	**Central Variant**	G C Band, E A Wrangham

'Perhaps the best route on the slab.' (1966 Interim guide) They finished up what is now the usual finish to Kirkus's Route. The original start was up Ordinary Route; the present means of entry provides a more consistent climb. The present finish was added by B Ingle and G Rogan on 12.5.66.

1952 June 22	**Reason in Revolt**	A J J Moulam, W R Craster
1952 July 3	**Pursuer's Folly**	P O Work, Miss R J Ruck
1952 July 5	**Ogof Direct**	A J J Moulam, G W S Pigott, W Bowman

A long-standing problem: the Ogof itself had been reached in 1935 by J P Copper et al.
The successful attempt began with seventeen people, most of whom were left at the Ogof when the ascent was completed late in the day. What became of them is not recorded. To lose one partner may be described as unfortunate. One is tempted to speculate that to lose fourteen was tactical rather than careless!
'The main challenge of this awe-inspiring face was taken up by many before the successful ascent. Most of those who failed finished up the upper part of Green Gully. Eight pitons were used on the first ascent and several are essential. At least one etrier has been found useful.' (1955 Supplement)
The more direct finish was added by H Smith, R Handley, C T Jones on 11 Aug 1956.
The aid had been reduced to two points by 1966; details of the first free ascent are unknown.

1953 April 15	**Toy Crack Climb**	P O Work, Miss R Busby
1953 April 15	**Anaconda**	P O Work, Miss R Busby
1953 Dec 31	**The Irish Mail**	G C Band, G J Sutton
1954 May 2	**May Rib**	T W Hughes, W Wynn
1954 May 9	**Tu Tin Tut**	M J Harris, J Neill, D Thomas

The first route in this, one of the loveliest of Welsh valleys.

1954 June 26	**Ivy Buttress**	G W S Pigott, W R Craster
1954 June 26	**Owl**	M J Harris, J Neill

Originally called Muddle by Oread parties. '…hard, vegetated and messy.'

1955 July 6	**Arrow Slab**	J O'Sullivan, T Williams
1955 July 6	**Cross Slab and Arête**	J O'Sullivan, T Williams
1955 Sept 3	**Tower of Strength**	M F W Holland, I C Bennett

The crack as now described was added by H I Banner, R G Wilson on 22.4.62 when they gave the climb its present name. The original name was Breakfast in Bed.

1955 Dec 24	**Slab Route**	F J Fisher, Miss B N Bird, D Penlington, Miss B Goodwin
1956 April 2	**Easter Wall**	J N Millward, P Janes, F Allen
1956 April 2	**Left Hand Route**	J N Millward, J Welbourne, P Janes
1956 May 26	**Bourdillon's Climb**	T D Bourdillon, H G Nichol (AL)

The first major artificial climb in the area. Several possible lines were tried in the vicinity before the final line succumbed. The pitons of the main pitch were very loose so Nichol, being the lighter of the two, completed it. The climb had been attempted on numerous previous occasions, and was initially named Briggs' Climb to commemorate an attempt by D H Briggs, D P Davis on 18.3.56 when a considerable height was attained. Fourteen pegs were used on the first ascent.

First Ascents 117

Probable second ascent in 5.70 with only six points of aid by R Evans, M Yates.
First free ascent by M Fowler, C Rowe in 1978.

1956 June 2 **Left Hand Route Direct**   R Handley, J N Millward
A2: the thin crack required two pitons.

1956 June 3 **Oak Tree Wall**   J N Millward, R Handley
1956 Aug 10 **Swept Wall**   J N Millward, Mrs M Millward
1956 Sept **Compression, Sunset Slabs**   A Neale, J Knowles
1958 May 26 **Jones's Traverse**   C T Jones, B D Wright, A Cowburn
The first two pitches had been climbed by C P Brown, J P Cooper on 4.8.46. The climb originally appeared as Girdle Traverse Right and continued across the Great Slab to finish up Direct Route.

1960 March 27 **Dwm**   J Brown, H Smith (3pts aid)
The start of modern climbing at Cidwm.
'Dwm was the hardest of the first routes, and it was hardly surprising that the great final roof yielded only with aid from pegs.' (New Climbs 1966)
Smith led the last pitch which was running with water and thus required aid. It is likely that less aid would have been needed if the rock had been dry.

1960 June 26 **Vertigo**   J Brown, B D Wright
The route started off as HVS with one point of aid, later got downgraded, and, 'thankfully' for most climbers, is back to its original grade.

1960 Sept 26 **The Curver**   J Brown, C T Jones
Another downgraded route, originally HVS, intimidated VS leaders for years; now upgraded.

1962 April 28 **Tramgo**   J Brown, C J S Bonington
The aid was two pegs and at least three slings. 'In 1962 Brown was back once more, this time to assault the overhangs on the right of Dwm. He climbed a fierce crack which splits several roofs, and called it Tramgo after the Tramgo Towers in the Andes [sic]. It was a fairly short but vicious route, and tales of the leader hanging horizontally by fist jams, and being unable to raise his hands above his head at the top were alarming to say the least.' (New Climbs 1966)
The route developed a tremendous reputation but seems to see few ascents. Unfortunately, the vegetation that builds up in the crack does not help matters.
First free ascent: J Moran, G Milburn, S Horrox on 1.6.78.

1962 April 28 **Hors d'œuvre**   C T Jones, C E Davies (AL)
1962 Oct 2 **Kangies Crawl**   A Wright, M Owen
1962 Oct 20 **Flintstone Rib**   B Ingle R G Wilson
1962 **Sideline**   R G Wilson, D Sanders
1963 May 18 **Penates**   B Ingle, R G Wilson
They began up the lower groove of Bourdillon's Climb. The final crack was added later in the year.

1963 May 25 **The Straighter**   J H Swallow, A Cowburn
'He had some trouble with the ascent in the middle of a rainstorm, and at last when he came down, the relief of his second, who sprained his ankle getting away from the crag, was short lived! Swallow was soon back with a replacement and completed the route in more favourable conditions.' (New Climbs 1966)
'Swallow had a fine year with his new route on Castell Cidwm and

made a contribution to the anti-peg movement by his second ascents of Agrippa on Craig yr Ysfa and The Groove on Llech Ddu, both with considerably less aid than on the first ascent. Unfortunately some of the younger generation cannot be said to be doing the same and keep setting precedents which some of us may find difficult to understand.' (P Crew, New Climbs 1964)

1963 June 1 **Crucible** B Ingle, R G Wilson
*One of the last great problems of the era. A fine piece of route-finding. The higher line was taken on the second pitch. With one point of aid; first free ascent unknown, but pre-1976.
'Undoubtedly the most important event of 1963 was Ingle's new route on Craig yr Ogof, Cwm Silyn. This route takes a superb line up a very improbable looking piece of rock and is comparable to Vector for quality and difficulty. It is to be hoped that this route will re-establish free climbing on Craig yr Ogof, which has been used for a long time as a peggers' playground. Most of the numerous confusing pegs in various parts of the cliff have now been removed.' (P Crew, New Climbs 1964)
From the above statement one may infer either that several artificial pitches had been climbed but either not recorded or not acknowledged, or that the pegs were the result of failed attempts at the large areas of unclimbed rock still remaining.*

1964 Sept 27 **Glwm** J Clements, A Bell (AL)
*With several points of aid. '… involved an alarming second pitch, traversing into the centre of the crag on loose pegs. That day it became clear that prusiks were an asset on Cidwm, for a peg came out on the second, and he found himself spinning in space 10 feet away from the nearest rock and unable to get back.' (New Climbs 1966)
The above description was sufficiently off-putting to deter not a few parties from setting foot on Castell Cidwm over the next eight years.
The present variation to pitch 2 was worked out by the same party in June 1965.*

1964 Oct 3 **Central Wall** A Bell, J Clements (AL)
*With two points of aid. The line had been spotted as a possible weakness up the wall but it had defeated quite a few strong parties prior to the first ascent.
First free ascent: W Wayman, T Jepson in 5.77*

1964 Oct 4 **Desifinado** R McHardy, B Ingle
Two pegs were used for protection on pitch 2. The variation was climbed by W S Lounds, D W Matthews on 5.4.69.

1964 Oct **The Ogof Traverse** B Ingle, P Crew, R McHardy.
The original name was Girdle Traverse Left to contrast with the name of the existing girdle (see 26.5.58). When the names were changed to their present ones is unclear.

1965 June 13 **The Erg** J Clements, R Beasley
*Aid consisted of a peg and sling on pitch 2 and slings and a peg on pitch 3.
Pitch 2 was climbed free by L R Holliwell, L E Holliwell in 1966.
First free ascent: R Fawcett, C Shorter in 4.80.*

1965 Oct **Eyrie** M Boysen, A Williams
1965 Oct **Cidwm Girdle** J Clements, D Potts
With six points of aid. 'Cidwm held one last problem – the Girdle.

At first glance it appeared impossible, but an assault ... showed the feasibility of the climb. The barrier proved to be the slab between The Straighter and The Erg. Clements fell off it once, but the complete route finally succumbed over two days in October, and was revealed as the most difficult undertaking on the cliff.'
(New Climbs 1966)
It was described in 1966 as *'Probably one of the most arduous undertakings in Wales. It is a formidable route of unrelenting difficulty and steepness traversing the crag from right to left. It is a high-level girdle, following geological weaknesses, with all the climbing in exhilarating positions.'*
Yet another description which would deter or unnerve subsequent parties.
First free ascent: P O'Donovan, P Williams (AL) on 12.8.83.
New Climbs 1966 commented that on Castell Cidwm 'Not much that is obvious remains for those with an eye for a new line: but this has so often been proved wrong in the past that who knows what the future holds?'

1966 March 19	**The Little Rocker**	D E Alcock, K J Wilson
1966 March 20	**Atropos**	M Boysen, A Williams, J Jordan

With one point of aid; first free ascent in 1976 by R Townshend and O Burroughs. 'That's a Boysen route. At least he wasn't a midget. With any luck there will be a move no one less than six-foot-four can do,' commented Burroughs not looking forward to following the shorter Townshend. (OUMJ, 1976-7)

1966 March 20	**Aquarius**	B Ingle, G Barrow.

They moved out onto the right wall half-way up the first pitch rejoining the corner some way above. The line as described was first climbed and named by M P Hatton, J A Maguire in 9.66 in ignorance of the first ascent.

1966 May 30	**Brutus**	B Ingle, G Barrow.

One of the noblest of them all. Two slings were used for aid on the first pitch. First free ascent unknown.

1966 Aug 22	**Helix**	R Edwards, E G Penman

With two points of aid; first recorded free ascent probably J Perrin & party in late 70s or early 80s.

1966 Aug 27	**Eureka**	L E Holliwell, L R Holliwell

The first of the Holliwells' impressive contributions to North Wales climbing.

1967 July 23	**Afterthought**	R Hughes, A J J Moulam
1968 June 9	**Codswallop**	R Evans

The rest of the party, who remain suspiciously anonymous, were unable to follow; it wasn't even raining so no excuses. A peg was used for tension to move left to the groove; first free ascent unknown. The first pitch had been climbed many years earlier.

1970 May 8	**Ignition**	C E M Yates, J Yates
1970 May 18	**Jabberwocky**	R Evans, J Yates, C E M Yates

Pitch 1 had been climbed previously by several parties. A peg was used for aid low in the groove; first claimed free ascent by J Hart, S Isherwood on 29.6.75. The main pitch was a well-known problem at the time.

1970 May 22	**Zip Groove**	R Evans, C E M Yates
1970 May 23	**Gotogo**	R D Kift, L W P Garland
1970 May 23	**West Arête**	C E M Yates, R Evans

120   *First Ascents*

1970 May 30	**Medicare, Poverty Street** J Gosling, G Macnair	
1970 June 13	**Green Gully** C E M Yates, J Yates	

It had been top-roped by E W Dance and others around 1952. Amazingly, summer gully lines kept getting climbed. This is perhaps the hardest gully in Wales.

1970 June 14   **Cysgodian Creep**   R Evans, C E M Yates
1970 Aug 15   **Resurrection**   J Perrin, N J Estcourt, C E M Yates

A fine discovery, which solved a long-standing problem that had been totally ignored by most climbers. Two pegs were used for aid while gardening. The 'gaunt red crag' first attempted in 1911 by Archer Thomson, who had written: 'A brief survey did not disclose to me any line of ascent up the face. We climbed the secondary edge on the left for some distance; then a very delicate traverse to the main edge was made in vain for this was found to be quite impossible.'

Erection, the true finishing-line, was finally added by H I Banner, J Yates, C E M Yates on 24.7.82.

Hellraiser was climbed by M Lewis, E Davies on 27.6.93

1970 Sept 19   **Guardian Angel**   C E M Yates, C T Jones, J Yates

With two points of aid; first claimed free ascent: M Crook, D Farrant on 30.6.84.

1970 Oct 18   **Dulyn Groove**   R Evans, B Wyvill

With several points of aid; first free ascent M Fowler, A Baker 20.6.82. A much-tried problem, the footholds on the arête at 30 metres having been reached on two previous occasions without aid.

1971 May 21   **Redog**   C E M Yates, J Yates

Not even guidebook work had put them off this cliff.

1971 June 22   **Yonec**   D P Owen, M H L Brewer, K Jones, R Evans
1971 June 22   **Spreadeagle**   K Jones, R Evans
1971 Sept 27   **The Schism**   C L Jones, D P Owen
1971 Sept 27   **Sundance**   M H L Brewer, K Jones

1971   **Cwm Silyn and Cwellyn by Mike Yates and Jim Perrin**

The first comprehensive and definitive guidebook exclusively dedicated to the area. In the early 60s, plans for a Snowdon West to match the South and East guides were somewhat undermined by the rising popularity of Clogwyn Du'r Arddu, which prompted its own volumes in 1963 and 1967 and the illustrated historical account of the crag's development in The Black Cliff..

1972 April 23   **Acrophily**   C H Taylor, M R Sinker (VL)
1974 Sept   **The Exterminating Angel/Efnisien**   J Perrin, D C O'Brien

Jim Perrin begins his recorded exploration of Cwm Pennant with a modern classic.

The second pitch was ascended as The Iconoclastic Exit by A Phizacklea and D Lampard on 31.7.87 and has been incorporated into this route to provide a more balanced climb. The original second pitch is now the upper part of Efnisien ('Enemies').

Variation start: by J Perrin, but now incorporated into Efnisien. 'I did the 5b crack start to Exterminating Angel solo before the route itself but thought it spoilt the latter, which is why it was never recorded.' (J Perrin)

First Ascents 121

1974		**Blood of the Raven, Copper Load, Er Cof, The Kite Flyer, Undelivered Sermon, Y Pregethwr** K Latham, G Dunne

Modern development begins on a blatantly obvious piece of rock. 'We also did some routes further down the valley but these were on very private land so we never went back for fear of being shot at!' (K Latham, referring to Clogwyn y Garreg). Er Cof is Welsh for 'in memoriam'.

1975 April	**The Second Coming** J Perrin, M Boysen
1975 May	**The Widening Gyre** J Perrin, P Doncaster

A gyre is a spiral or helix.

1975	**The Ceremony of Innocence** J Perrin, I Nightingale
c.1975	**Grave Matters** J Perrin
1976 May	**Mere Anarchy** M Boysen, J Perrin
1978 May 29	**Blood on the Tracks** C E M Yates, H I Banner
1979 Aug	**Zwm** F Crook, K Crook
1980 April 8	**Hang 'em High** J Moran, G Milburn

The first of the super-routes to go. Unfortunately for the first-ascent team, the wind was at gale force and neither fancied hanging around for any of the other superb lines that were so obviously waiting to be done.

1981 Aug 2	**Slopey** H I Banner, C E M Yates
1982 June 15	**Bandersnatch** M Fowler, A Baker
1982 Aug 14	**Zarquon** H I Banner, C E M Yates
1983 Feb 24	**Menna** M Lewis, E Davies
1983 June	**Oars Moses** J Sylvester

For years, locals had spoken about a technical arête of John's in the Nantlle quarries but no one knew where it was. Reclaimed by M Lewis, E Davies as Y Gododdin, 26.9.92 at E2 5c!

1984 Aug 23	**Flashback** M Lewis, B Grimston, E Davies
1986 Oct 31	**Neglected Partner** C Parkin, P Hawkins

Acting on a note in the minor crags section of the 1971 guide, though unaware of the 1974 activity, climbers began again the development of the closest crag to the road in this guide. The 1974 routes were also reascended and renamed, but the original names have been retained.

1986 Oct	**Pearly Dew Drops Drop** P Hermes, L Coles

Sadly, chipped.

1986 Nov 2	**Left in Tears, Right Bastard** G Smith, C Parkin

The second ascent of the former was an on-sight solo by P Pritchard.

1986 Nov 2	**Line of Best Fit** D Towse, M Crook (both led)
1986	**Skittle Alley** G Smith
1987 July 31	**The Seraphic Sanction, The Killing Fields, Day of Reckoning** D Lampard, A Phizacklea (AL)

The busiest day for new routes seen on Craig Cwm Trwsgl. Lampard and Phizacklea clean up on the fine dolerite buttresses around The Exterminating Angel.

1988 May 10	**Balance of Power, Potency** P R Littlejohn, J de Montjoye

Two tremendous routes that were to inspire Littlejohn to drag Cidwm into the 80s. The former was a bold on-sight lead.
'Pat had abbed the line [of Potency] and placed a peg the previous week. Worries of inadequate protection were starting to bother him even as we drove over from the Gwynant. His reasoning was

	that, as the crux was going to be gaining the peg, he should place another, lower. It was, he didn't.
1988 May 27	**Heading for Heights** P R Littlejohn, J de Montjoye
	'We were still pumped from the previous day, having climbed two new routes at Hyll Drem. Pat knew that there were good holds to go for, but he thought that his only hope of reaching them was to jump. He got them statically. The strong bastard.'
1988 June 4	**Dwmsday** S Monks, P R Littlejohn (AL)
1988 June 5	**Glasnost** P R Littlejohn, S Monks (AL)
1988 June 5	**Light Years** P R Littlejohn
1988 Aug 6	**The Bodysnatchers** S Howe, I A Jones
1988 Oct 22	**Equinox** P R Littlejohn, T Jepson
1989 May 11	**Bombproof Runner** C Phillips, J Tombs
	Leaving everything to the imagination, the 1989 guidebook declared: 'An E3 5c on the third outcrop from the road.' Not content with this, it mentioned no hint of which road to start from!
1989 May 11	**Nordor** D Lampard, D Green, I A Jones.
	The last man climbed the route by the light from South Stack lighthouse! As usual, naming the route proved harder than the climbing of it. The team, as is their wont, sought inspiration by retiring to a local hostelry. During a game of darts a stray arrow gave them the vision they needed. The following day the leader changed his mind and called the route Red Shift, sent off the details, then, too late, changed his mind again. Correctness restored.
1989 June	**Howl at the Moon** M Turner, S McRory
	Hard modern climbing comes to Cwellyn.
1989	**Tremadog and Cwm Silyn by Mark Pretty, Dave Farrant, and Geoff Milburn**
	The Cwm Silyn [and Cwellyn] section was written by Farrant with Historical by Milburn.
1992 Aug 2	**Blodeuwedd** M Lewis, J Yates
1992 Sept 11	**Erwaint** M Lewis, J Yates, E Davies
	A couple of non-slate slate-routes.
1992	**The Great and Secret Show** D Dutton, I Lloyd-Jones
1992	**Ian's Route** I Lloyd-Jones, D Dutton
	A couple of sport climbs for the boys. The first ascensionists did not record the routes for two years, by which time they had forgotten nearly all the details!
1992	**Blinded by the Light** I Lloyd-Jones, C Stephenson
1993 May	**Walter Buffalo** G Smith, M Crook (on sight)
1993	**Hanging Gardens of Demijohn** B McMurray
	Four bolts in 5 metres in a poor quarry – was it worth it!
1994 Aug 21	**The Circus Animals' Desertion** J Perrin, Z P Leppert
1995 May 4	**The Arrow** M Lewis, J Yates
1995 May 5	**The Legend of Johnny Toto** M Crook, J Tombs
1995 May 20	**Schwept** C Phillips, T Millichamp
1995 May 22	**The Sceptic** P R Littlejohn, E Cooper
	'The groove left of Guardian Angel, which terminates in a cornice of loose blocks, has been left for the next generation (with full body armour).' (1989 guidebook) What's Pat got that the rest of us don't know about?

First Ascents 123

1995 June	**The End of History**	M Crook, G Smith

A mere forty-seven years between the previous first ascent on this cliff and this addition – it may well be that long before there is another!

1995 July 10	**Sweeper**	C Phillips, L Develin
1995 Aug 16	**Good Golly Miss Molly, Shake, Rattle, and Roll**	Z P Leppert, M A Kellas
1996 June 27	**Freedwm Roof**	S Myles, C Lowry

The hardest route in the guide.

1996 Sept 1	**Another Green World, Chantilly Lace**	Z P Leppert, M A Kellas
1996 Sept 5	**The Walkers' Pair**	M E Crook, J R Toombs

'For connoisseurs only.' (M Crook)

1996	**Indefinite Article**	T Keep, J Bertalot
1997 March 31	**Y Credwr**	P R Littlejohn, H Clarke

Once again Pat proves that there is rock to be had in the most unlikely of places. The name is Welsh for 'The Believer'.

1997 April 16	**Voice in the Wilderness**	P R Littlejohn, T Jepson (VL on sight)
1997 July 21	**Bronwen, Ffion Gwyn**	P Jenkinson, I A Jones
1997 Aug 10	**Lazing on a Sunny Afternoon**	Z P Leppert, L McGinley
1997 Sept 21	**The Man in White, Lies, Damn Lies and Statistics, Out! Out! Out!, Up Your Hacienda!, Glorified Barmen with Attitude, Turf Wars, Sod's Corner, The Windtakers, Ken's Crack, The Magic Sod**	I A Jones, G Fenton

Some of these routes may have been done before as the crag has certainly received attention in years past, though nothing has been recorded (see note under 1974, page 121). The first few route-names recall personalities and events surrounding the May 1997 general election.

1997	**The Ivy League**	I A Jones, R E Wightman

Possibly climbed before, as a jammed hex was found high in the corner, but not recorded. The name refers to a libellous statement that appeared in a magazine article concerning the over-enthusiastic cleaning of crags.

1998 May 15	**The Devils**	P R Littlejohn
1998 June 12	**Summer Buttress**	P R Littlejohn
1999 Sept 26	**Kelled Crack**	K Neal, M Lewis
1999 Sept 26	**Vladophobia**	M Lewis, K Neal

A made-up name implying a fear of being impaled.

2000 May 13	**Lliwedd Comes to Llechog**	J Hope, K Neal (AL)
2000 May 13	**Plant y Fflam**	M Lewis, J Yates, J Hope, K Neal
2000 May 13	**A Taste of Honey**	M Lewis, J Yates
2000 June 17	**Y Bwbach Llwyd**	M Lewis, J Yates

This is the ghost that is said to haunt Snowdon.

2000 July 22	**Diwrnod I'r Brenin**	M Lewis, J Yates

Literally: 'Day for the King' – a good enjoyable time. Mike was doing the route as a birthday treat for Judy – if only all our partners were so easily pleased!

2000 July 22	**Skirmish, The Man Who Shot a Fox**	J Hope, K Neal
2000 July 22	**Future Tense**	K Neal, J Hope
2000 Aug	**Cities of Red Night**	A Wainwright, M Crook
2000 Aug	**Natty Dread, Spectrum**	J Appleby, H Drasdo
2001 June 23	**Gambit**	J Hope, K Neal
2001 June 26	**After the Goldrush**	M Lewis

2001 Aug 28	**Strange Fruit**	M Lewis, J Hope
2001 Aug 28	**The Pickpocket**	J Hope, M Lewis
2001 Sept 10	**Titanium Rib**	P Jenkinson, T Taylor
2001 Sept 10	**The Spies Came out of the Water**	T Taylor, P Jenkinson
2001 Sept 17	**Arabian Flights, Doctor Butt Says It's Easy, Mr Whippy, Tea with the Taliban, The Full Trash Can, Whose Skyline Is It Anyway** P Jenkinson, T Taylor
2001 Sept 17	**Get a Sandal on This, Scarab Hunting, The Brown Runnel, Running out of Rock** T Taylor, P Jenkinson
2001 Sept 23	**While the Cat's Away** J Hope, K Neal
2001 Sept 25	**Terry's Rump** T Taylor, P Jenkinson (both solo)
2001 Sept 25	**Wish I Could Be Elsewhere** T Taylor, P Jenkinson

An attempt was made to develop a much neglected crag. After one route they ran away.

2001 Sept	**Jug Rehab, Nexus**	G Smith, M Crook
2002 March 12	**Deaf School**	J Appleby, G Peters
2002 March 12	**Buzzard Groove**	G Peters, J Appleby
2002 June 18	**Birth of Gravity, Dark Summer, Wild Wind** T Taylor, J Appleby
2002 June 18	**Song for A Taylor** J Appleby, T Taylor
2002 Aug 23	**The Mellow Misogynist** M Lewis, J Yates
2002 Sept 7	**Talaq, Talaq, Talaq** P Jenkinson, T Taylor
2002 Sept 7	**Tropical Rain Rib** T Taylor, P Jenkinson
2002 Sept 21	**Not Taylor Made** P Jenkinson, T Taylor
2002 Sept 21	**No More Flaying, No More Slaying** T Taylor, P Jenkinson
2002 Sept 21	**Ar y Drwm, Fair and Squaw, Ni Yd'r Indians** P Jenkinson (on-sight solo)
2002 Sept 21	**More to Gain, No More Playing, Tomahawk** T Taylor (on-sight solo)
2002 Sept	**Cruppered** T Taylor, P Jenkinson
2003 April 21	**Del Cap Corner, Extreme Unction** P Jenkinson, T Taylor
2003 May 9	**Vortex of Desire, The Pleasures of Wind, The Plump Principle, Gael Forces, Gael in a Gale, Del Niño, Spinning in the Wind, Plinthing for Beginners** T Taylor

All solo except The Plump Principle (unseconded) and Del Niño (seconded by D Owen). See also note under 21.9.97 – the same may apply.

2003 June 28	**Terry Tomb Tome** T Taylor (solo)
2003 June 28	**In Search of Perpetual Motion** T Taylor, P Jenkinson (both solo)
2003 June 28	**Another Day, To Rest Is to Rust, Play It Smooth** P Jenkinson, T Taylor

Index of Climbs

Acrophily	36
Adam Rib	23
After the Goldrush	43
Afterthought	84
Amphitheatre Gully	83
Anaconda	95
Angel Pavement	55
Another Day	57
Another Green World	46
Aquarius	82
Ar y Drwm	101
Arabian Flights	92
Arrow Slab	38
Arrow, The	106
Artist's Climb	73
Atropos	85
Balance of Power	31
Bandersnatch	76
Bankers' Buttress	70
Bar Steward, The	46
Batelion	46
Bedrock Gully	86
Bending Groove	95
Birth of Gravity	100
Black Gully	72
Black Rib	42
Blinded by the Light	108
Blodeuwedd	52
Blood of the Raven	63
Blood on the Tracks	43
Bodysnatchers, The	88
Bombproof Runner	102
Bourdillon's Climb	78
Broad Gully	70
Bronwen	63
Brown Runnel, The	93
Brutus	74
Buzzard Crack	102
Buzzard Groove	99
Bwbach Llwyd, Y	42
Caterpillar	95
Central Rib	39
Central Ridge	42
Central Variant	80
Central Wall	31
Ceremony of Innocence, The	109
Chantilly Lace	46
Chasm, The	104
Chinaman	97
Cidwm Girdle	34
Circus Animals' Desertion, The	40
Cities of Red Night	27
Cloister Climb, The	41
Codswallop	77
Colin's Gully	87
Compression	96
Copper Load	63
Cracks, The	104
Credwr, Y	55
Cross Slab and Arête	39
Crucible	77
Cruppered	59
Curver, The	29
Cysgodian Creep	87
Dark Summer	100
Day of Reckoning	108
Deaf School	99
Deep Chimney	67
Defcon Stacks	51
Del Cap Corner	29
Del Niño	58
Desifinado	75
Devils, The	54
Direct Route	80
Diwrnod I'r Brenin	42
Dobbin	27
Doctor Butt Says It's Easy	93
Dulyn Groove	88
Dwm	33
Dwmsday	33
Easter Wall	104
Eastern Arête	60
Eastern Gutter	40
Ebon Ridge	87
Efnisien	107
End of History, The	61
Engineers' Climb	69
Equinox	30
Er Cof	62
Erection	41
Erg, The	30
Erwaint	52
Eureka	76
Eve's Folly	23
Explorers' Traverse	98
Exterminating Angel, The	107
Extreme Unction	29
Eyrie	85
Fair and Squaw	101
Ffion Gwyn	63
Finale Wall	35
Fingercrack, The	99
Five Cave Gully	43
Flashback	97
Flintstone Rib	86
Four-Pitch Gully	85
Fox Route	26
Freedwm	33
Full Trash Can, The	92
Future Tense	45
Gael Forces	58
Gael in a Gale	58
Gambit	39
Gardener's Gully	67
Get a Sandal on This	92
Glasnost	32
Glorified Barmen with Attitude	58
Glwm	32

Index

Glyndŵr's Ladder	94
Good Golly Miss Molly	46
Gotogo	84
Grass Pitch Gully	26
Grave Matters	102
Great and Secret Show, The	52
Great Arête, The	52
Green Gully	72
Greenhouse Roof, The	46
Grey Gully and Wall	44
Guardian Angel	56
Handcrack, The	99
Hang 'em High	34
Hanging Gardens of Demijohn	49
Heading for Heights	31
Heather Rib	71
Helix	109
Hellraiser	41
Hors d'œuvre	35
Howl at the Moon	34
Ian's Route	52
Ignition	96
In Search of Perpetual Motion	59
Indefinite Article	107
Irish Mail	89
Ivy Buttress	104
Ivy League, The	102
Jabberwocky	77
Jericho	84
Jezebel	23
Jones's Traverse	73
Jug Rehab	48
Kangies Crawl	82
Kelled Crack	66
Ken's Crack	59
Killing Fields, The	107
Kirkus's Direct	81
Kirkus's Route	81
Kitchen Rake, The	86
Kite Flyer, The	62
Knight's Move Climb	24
L.M.H.	70
Lamb's Leap	36
Lazing on a Sunny Afternoon	47
Left in Tears	62
Left-Hand Route	103
Left-Hand Route Direct	103
Legend of Johnny Toto, The	27
Leo's Wall	26
Lichen Ridge	26
Lies, Damn Lies, and Statistics	58
Light Years	29
Line of Best Fit	49
Little Kitchen, The	86
Little Rocker, The	47
Lliwedd Comes to Llechog	43
Lodestone	95
Loosenard	89
Magic Sod, The	57
Maidan Buttress	97
Maidan Gully	97
Mallory's Ridge	61
Man in White, The	59
Man Who Shot a Fox, The	45
Manchester Rib	25
May Rib	94
Medicare	24
Mellow Misogynist, The	66
Menna	104
Mere Anarchy	108
Mermaid Climb, The	40
More to Gain	101
Mr Whippy	93
Mystery II, The	36
Nadroedd	46
Natty Dread	100
Neglected Partner	62
Nexus 6	48
Ni Ydy'r Indians	101
Nirvana Wall	72
No Highway	54
No More Flaying	101
No More Gain	100
No More Playing	101
No More Slaying	101
Non-Engineers' Climb	69
Nordor	88
North Buttress	64
North Gully, The	45
Not Taylor Made	100
Oak Tree Wall	105
Oars Moses	52
Oblique Route	75
Ogof Direct	74
Ogof Traverse, The	78
Omega	95
Oppenauer Slab	27
Ordinary Route	80
Original Route	83
Out! Out! Out!	59
Outside Edge Route	79
Overhanging Chimneys	68
Owl	103
Pearly Dew Drops Drop	49
Penates	78
Pickpocket, The	38
Pink Slab	98
Pinnacle Ridge	57
Pis-Aller Rib	25
Plant y Fflam	43
Play It Smooth	59
Pleasures of Wind, The	58
Plinthing for Beginners	59
Potency	30
Poverty Street	24
Pregethwr, Y	62
Primrose Path	56
Prow Gully	70
Pump Principle, The	58
Purple Tailed Love Fish	51
Pursuer's Folly	94
Quest for Corbeau	89
Raven Buttress	27
Reason in Revolt	53
Recess Route, The	67
Redog	96
Residents' Wall	47
Resurrection	40

Reunion Cracks	60
Rib and Tower	83
Right Bastard	62
Running out of Rock	93
Saxifrage Rib	25
Scarab Hunting	92
Scarf, The	68
Sceptic, The	56
Schism, The	102
Schwept	105
Second Coming, The	109
Sentries' Ridge	57
Seraphic Sanction, The	107
Shake, Rattle, and Roll	47
Sideline	86
Skirmish	45
Skittle Alley	62
Slab and Groove	45
Slab Route	103
Slopey	45
Sod's Corner	59
Song for A Taylor	100
South Buttress	63
Spectrum	100
Spies Came out of the Water, The	92
Spinning in the Wind	58
Spreadeagle	105
Straighter, The	30
Strange Fruit	38
Summer Buttress	47
Sundance	103
Sunset Rib	71
Sunset Slabs	44
Sweep Wall	86
Sweeper	104
Swept Wall	105
Talaq Talaq Talaq	100
Taste of Honey, A	43
Tea with the Taliban	92
Tension Crack	95
Terror Infirmer	68
Terry Tomb Tome	57
Terry's Rump	99
Titanium Rib	92
To Rest Is to Rust	59
Tomahawk	101
Torpedo Route	39
Tower Chimney	68
Tower of Strength	84
Toy Crack Climb	98
Tramgo	33
Trinity Buttress B	44
Trinity Buttress C	44
Tropical Rain Rib	100
Tu Tin Tut	106
Turf Wars	59
Two Chimney Route	98
Undelivered Sermon	63
Up Your Hacienda	58
Upper Slab Climb	82
Vertigo	31
Vladophobia	66
Voice in the Wilderness	54
Vortex of Desire	58
Walkers' Pair, The	64
Wall, The	99
Walter Buffalo	34
West Arête	83
While the Cat's Away	39
Whose Skyline Is It Anyway	92
Widening Gyre, The	108
Wild Wind	100
Windtakers, The	59
Wish I Could Be Elsewhere	94
Wolf's Buttress	35
Yellow Buttress	25
Yonec	103
Zarquon	41
Zip Groove	88
Zwm	32

Index of Winter Climbs

Amphitheatre Gully	83
Aquarian Wall	82
Atrocity Run	73
Bedrock Gully	86
Black Gully	72
Broad Gully	70
Central Ice Falls	90
Cleaver, The	89
Colin's Gully	87
Final Cut, The	89
Four-Pitch Gully	85
Great Stone Shoot, The	84
Heart of Ice	90
Ice Mamba	90
Little Kitchen, The	86
Main Left-Hand Gully	64
Mask of Death	86
Mr Drainpipe of Stockport	90
Prow Gully	70
Rake End Wall	90
White Snake	83
Widow of the Web, The	84

Accident Procedure

First Aid
If spinal or head injuries are suspected, do not move the patient without skilled help, except to maintain breathing or if this is essential for further protection.

If breathing has stopped, clear the airways and start artificial respiration. Do not stop until the patient recovers or expert opinion has diagnosed death.

Summon help as quickly as is compatible with safety. Do not hesitate or delay.

Rescue
In the event of an accident where further assistance is required, dial 999 and ask for the Police. The Police are responsible for co-ordinating all rescues and will contact other services as necessary.
- State that you require cliff rescue and report the exact location (six-figure grid reference if possible) and details of the accident.
- Be prepared to give your own name and home address if asked.
- Follow any further instructions or requests issued.

Helicopter
In the event of a Helicopter evacuation, all climbers on or off the cliff should take heed. A helicopter flying close to the cliff will make verbal communication very difficult and small stones will be dislodged by the rotor downdraught. All loose equipment should be secured and climbers in precarious positions should try to make themselves safe.

The people with the injured person should try to identify their location. **No** attempt should be made to throw a rope at the helicopter, but assistance should be given to the helicopter crew if requested. Do not approach until directions are given by the crew. In particular, keep well clear of the main rotor, the tail rotor, and the engine exhaust.

Follow-up
After an accident, a report has to be compiled. Normally the details will be collated at the scene by the Police or rescue team, who will then pass the information to the Mountain Rescue Council Statistics Officer.

If unreasonable equipment failure is suspected then the British Mountaineering Council's technical committee may wish to investigate; contact the BMC at 177-179 Burton Road, West Didsbury, Manchester, M20 2BB. In the event of a serious accident, any equipment used by the casualty may be impounded.

Local Hospitals
The nearest Accident and Emergency unit is Ysbytty Gwynedd, Bangor.

CLIMBING GUIDES TO WALES

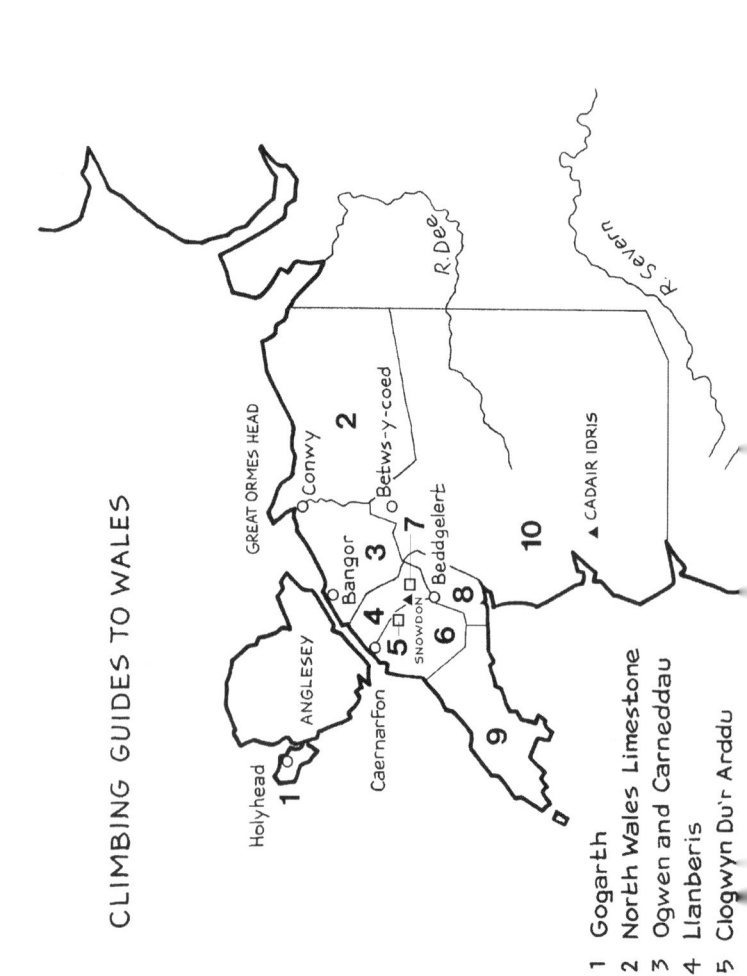

1 Gogarth
2 North Wales Limestone
3 Ogwen and Carneddau
4 Llanberis
5 Clogwyn Du'r Arddu